BASICS

INTERIOR ARCHITECTURE

04

elements/
objects

Ethical: awareness/ reflect-ion/ debate

ava academia

An AVA Book

Published by AVA Publishing SA
Rue des Fontenailles 16
Case Postale
1000 Lausanne 6
Switzerland

Tel: +41 786 005 109
Email: enquiries@avabooks.ch

Distributed by Thames & Hudson (ex-North America)
181a High Holborn
London WC1V 7QX
United Kingdom

Tel: +44 20 7845 5000
Fax: +44 20 7845 5055
Email: sales@thameshudson.co.uk
www.thamesandhudson.com

Distributed in the USA and Canada by:
Ingram Publisher Services Inc.
1 Ingram Blvd
La Vergne TN 37086
USA

Tel: +1 866 400 5351
Fax: +1 800 838 1149
Email:
customer.service@ingrampublisherservices.com

English Language Support Office
AVA Publishing (UK) Ltd.

Tel: +44 1903 204 455
Email: enquiries@avabooks.ch

ISBN : 978-2-940411-10-8

10 9 8 7 6 5 4 3 2 1

Design by John F McGill

Production by :
AVA Book Production Pte. Ltd., Singapore

Tel: +65 6334 8173
Fax: +65 6259 9830
Email: production@avabooks.com.sg

Elements/Objects

Name:
Joyn office system
(see pp 124+125)

Location:
N/A

Date:
2002

Designer:
Bouroullec Brothers

Contents

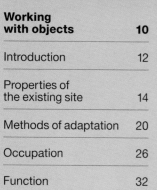

Elements/Objects

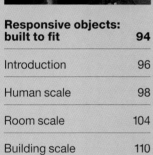

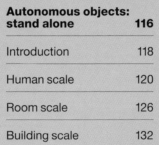

Contents

The aim of this book is to provide a clear, comprehensible and enlightening investigation into the practice of designing interior space. The focus of this study will be upon the objects and elements that occupy this space. It will discuss the manner in which they are designed, the need for functional considerations, the materials from which they are constructed and, of course, scale, as well as examining the methods by which a distinct relationship is created between the object and the interior space that it occupies.

A purposely-placed object or element (the two terms are interchangeable in the context of this book) has a definite relationship with the space that it inhabits, whether that is the decaying

Whether the designer is adapting an existing structure or occupying a new building, the methods of organising the elements within the space are not dissimilar. The designer needs to be aware of such contextual issues as the shape and size of the space, the possibilities for natural and artificial light, opportunities for making connections, whether these are physical or visual, as well as being aware of any structural constraints. A careful analysis of the proposed space will provide many clues that will aid the designer in the creation of the new interior.

How to get the most out of this book

This book introduces different aspects of the organisation of interior space via dedicated chapters for each topic. Each chapter provides clear examples from leading architectural practices, annotated to explain the reasons behind the design choices made.

Section headers
Each chapter is broken down into sub-sections, the title of which can be found at the top left-hand corner of each spread.

Section introduction
Each sub-section is introduced by a short paragraph, outlining the content to be covered.

Page numbers
Page numbers are displayed in the top right-hand corner of each spread.

Elements and objects of a fairly large scale generally act in one of two ways. The first is as a freestanding or independent object; this may take the form of a complete room or function. The second is an element that serves to tie a series of distinct areas or actions together. This could be a complete floor, a wall or an element, which changes as it flows through a space.

Above:
The bar counter
The aesthetic of the bar was directly influenced by car tail lights racing through the night-time streets outside.

Grand Central bar

Name:
Grand Central bar
Location:
London, England
Date:
2001
Designer:
Block Architecture

A single element can tie a number of different spaces and activities together. Grand Central is situated in a high, L-shaped space on a busy corner site in Shoreditch, London. The oddly shaped interior forms a collection of dissimilar spaces rather than one united space. This condition was exploited by the designers to generate a series of little areas, each with varying degrees of intimacy. The designers tied all the separate spaces together with a single flowing element. A wall of light seems to drift around the wine bar. It begins and ends at the door, running around the space, separating and defining the distinct areas.

The designers describe this as a process that uses light, movement and electricity as physical building elements, to create an environment based on city flux. They were influenced by long exposure photography of traffic flow. The light-stream walls are constructed from strips of live edge and coloured Perspex that have been laminated together and back-lit. This imitates the effect of the extruded light paths produced by the head and tail lights of passing cars.

Although the wall that runs through the space is broken, it appears to be a complete element that unites the disparate spaces within the room.

Above:
The bar
The wall of light races around the space.

Live edge perspex
Live edge perspex is a sheet polymer that contains fluorescent dyes. Light is transmitted through the sheet, and is much more intense at the edges. If lit from one side, the other edge appears to glow.

Responsive objects: built to fit

Human scale > **Room scale** > Building scale

Chapter footers
The current chapter is displayed in the bottom left-hand corner of each spread.

Boxed texts
Additional points of interest to the reader are displayed in grey boxes.

The examples shown include a mix of photographs, sketches and drawings, which, when combined with a detailed analysis in the text, create a unique and fascinating insight into the world of interior architecture.

Pull quotes
Additional quotes from subject experts and practitioners.

Case study information
Each case study is introduced by name, location, date and designer.

Room scale

108+**109**

'Denari has been a leader in his generation's use of advanced technology to propose architecture that shifts, bends, folds and unfolds, always challenging conventional geometry with pure beauty and a quality he refers to as "cultural sustainability".'

Neil M. Denari

l.a. Eyeworks

Name:
l.a. Eyeworks

Location:
Los Angeles, USA

Date:
2002

Designer:
Neil M. Denari Architects (NMDA)

Neil M. Denari Architects have a reputation for creating innovative and exciting design solutions. Whatever the particular functional requirements of a project, they regard each commission as an experiment that attempts to redirect expectations toward new and even better forms of functional and aesthetic performance.

The vision for the l.a. Eyeworks store in Los Angeles was based upon a balance between the conventional demands of a commercial retail practice and the dynamic identity of the fashion company. This design satisfies all the normal retail requirements, such as the need for a transparent window display, sales and display counters and signage. However this is achieved with one gracefully twisting sinuous element. A gaseous blue surface winds its way though the length of the shop, changing its form, alignment and purpose as it goes. It performs many functions: perforated ceiling plane; window display; bench; shelving unit and sales counter.

The design of this multifunctional element shapes space and movement though a continuous suspended surface. It is both efficient and inventive. It merges the functional demands of an eyewear store with the ambitions of high fashion.

Above:
The reception
The counter is integral to the linear folding element.

Facing page:
Retail space
The organic element rolls through the space before folding down to become a display counter.

Responsive objects: built to fit

Human scale – **Room scale** – Building scale

Captions
All captions carry a directional and title for easy reference.

Section footers
Past, present and future sub-sections are listed in the bottom right-hand corner of each spread. The current sub-section is highlighted in bold.

How to get the most out of this book

The design of a new interior and the remodelling of an existing building are approached in a similar manner. Interior architecture and design is a complex process of understanding the qualities of the existing or proposed building while simultaneously combining these factors with the functional requirements of end-users. Every interior is populated with a series of related objects. These may be freestanding or fitted, handmade or constructed in a factory, large or small. It is the careful distribution of these, based upon a discriminating reading of the space to be occupied and a thorough knowledge of the needs of the end-users, that creates an interior of consequence and worth.

Name:
Boekhandel Selexyz Dominicanen
(see pp 016+017)

Location:
Maastricht, Netherlands

Date:
2007

Designer:
Merkx + Girod

Properties of the existing site

A careful analysis of the host building will reveal a number of key characteristics and particular properties, all of which have an influence upon the significant strategic arrangement of the interior space. These discoveries may be as simple as an acknowledgement of the sun's path, the main direction of the circulation or the structural system of the building. Of course, the analysis may uncover considerably more complex contextual, structural or historical factors, all of which can contribute to the new interior.

Methods of adaptation

The existing building can be remodelled in a number of different ways, with varying degrees of permanence. The remodelling can range from complete and irretrievable alterations to the space to the temporary placement of moveable objects. Museum design, for example, is typical of permanent remodelling, while the design of an exhibition is representative of the more ephemeral approach.

Occupation

The new users of an interior space will have a number of programmatic requirements, all of which have to be satisfied by the designer. Those who occupy the remodelled or newly designed space need to feel that they own it and that it has been designed specifically for them.

Function

The creation of a space that serves the needs of the end-users of the interior is the ultimate objective of all designers. The programmatic requirements of the proposed function need to be examined thoroughly to ensure that there is a definite compatibility between the existing building and the new function.

Facing page:
The CaixaForum, Madrid, Spain (see pp 018+019).

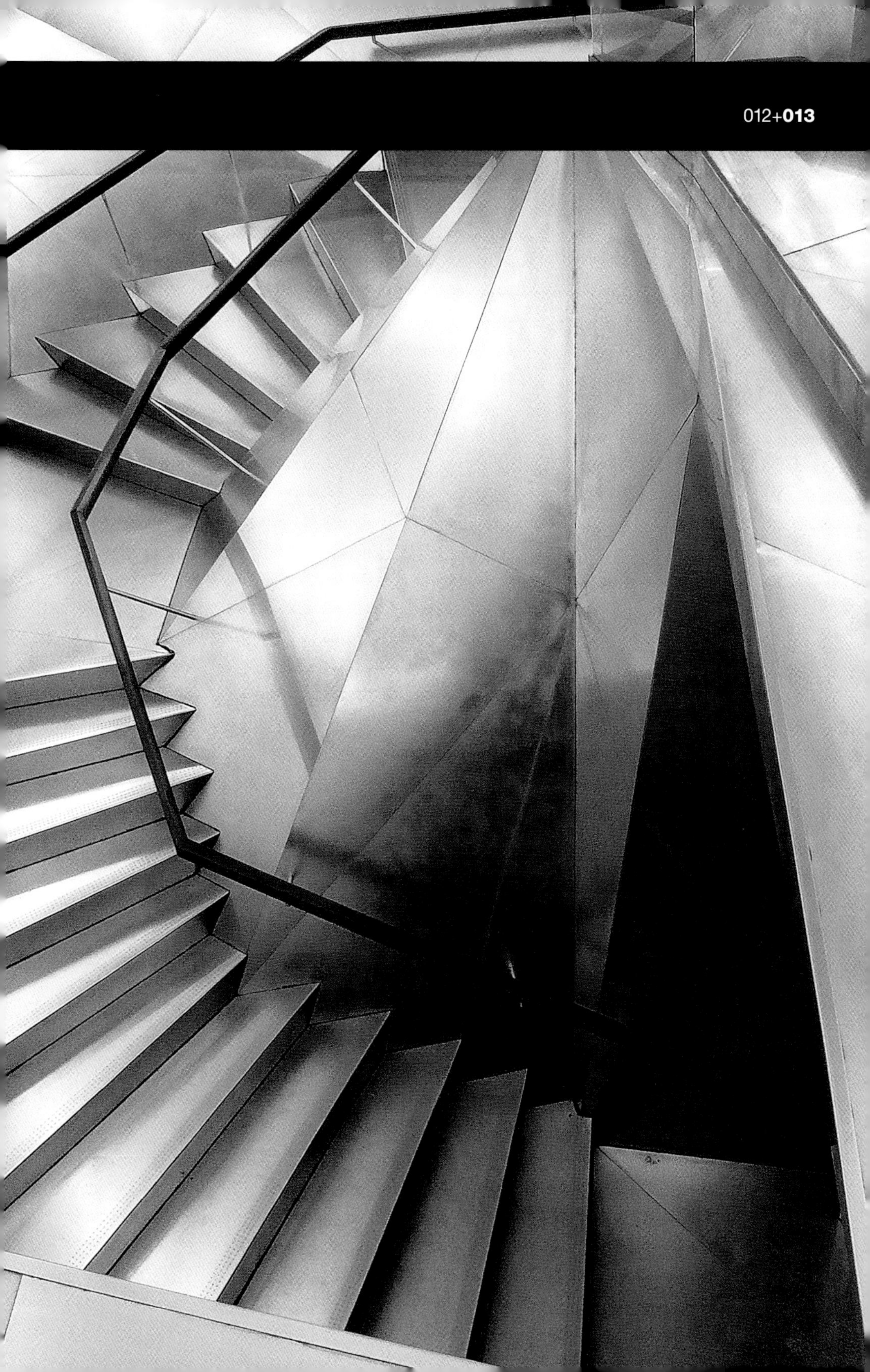

The designer can analyse the nature, characteristics and qualities of the existing building. This examination can then help to inform the redesign of the spaces. The elegance and rhythm of an existing building can provide the organisational impetus for the redesign of the interior. The regularity of the structure may provide the necessary sense of order that will control the placements of new elements within the space.

Facing page:
Display fittings
The Georgian-style containers reflect Givenchy's exquisite trademark tailoring.

Givenchy boutique

Name:
Givenchy boutique

Location:
Paris, France

Date:
2008

Designer:
Jamie Fobert Architects

The very rigid structural organisation of the original building has aided the designer in the arrangement of this series of beautifully designed objects in this new store. Jamie Fobert has attempted to capture the elegance and craftsmanship of Givenchy's history while creating a contemporary spatial experience for the shopper. Through the careful placement of a small number of beautifully crafted objects, the designer has created an atmosphere of serenity and calm. This is combined with a quirky reference to history, resulting in an interior with a suggestion of tradition mixed with contemporary design.

The shop interior is populated with a series of open rooms. These contain the display fittings for the clothes. The language of these units reflects the exquisite tailoring that is Givenchy's trademark. They are both traditional and modern. The wooden panelling alludes to Georgian drawing rooms, while the fragmented openness of the units is a reference to the architectural promenade of modernism.

These beautifully crafted objects are arranged in strict lines, based upon the organisation of the building, especially the window pattern. The openings are fully glazed with minimal frames and no window display; this creates long uninterrupted views into the interior. The containers are organised in lines behind the solid structural uprights and so are partially hidden. This adds to the modest, slightly reserved and demure quality of the boutique.

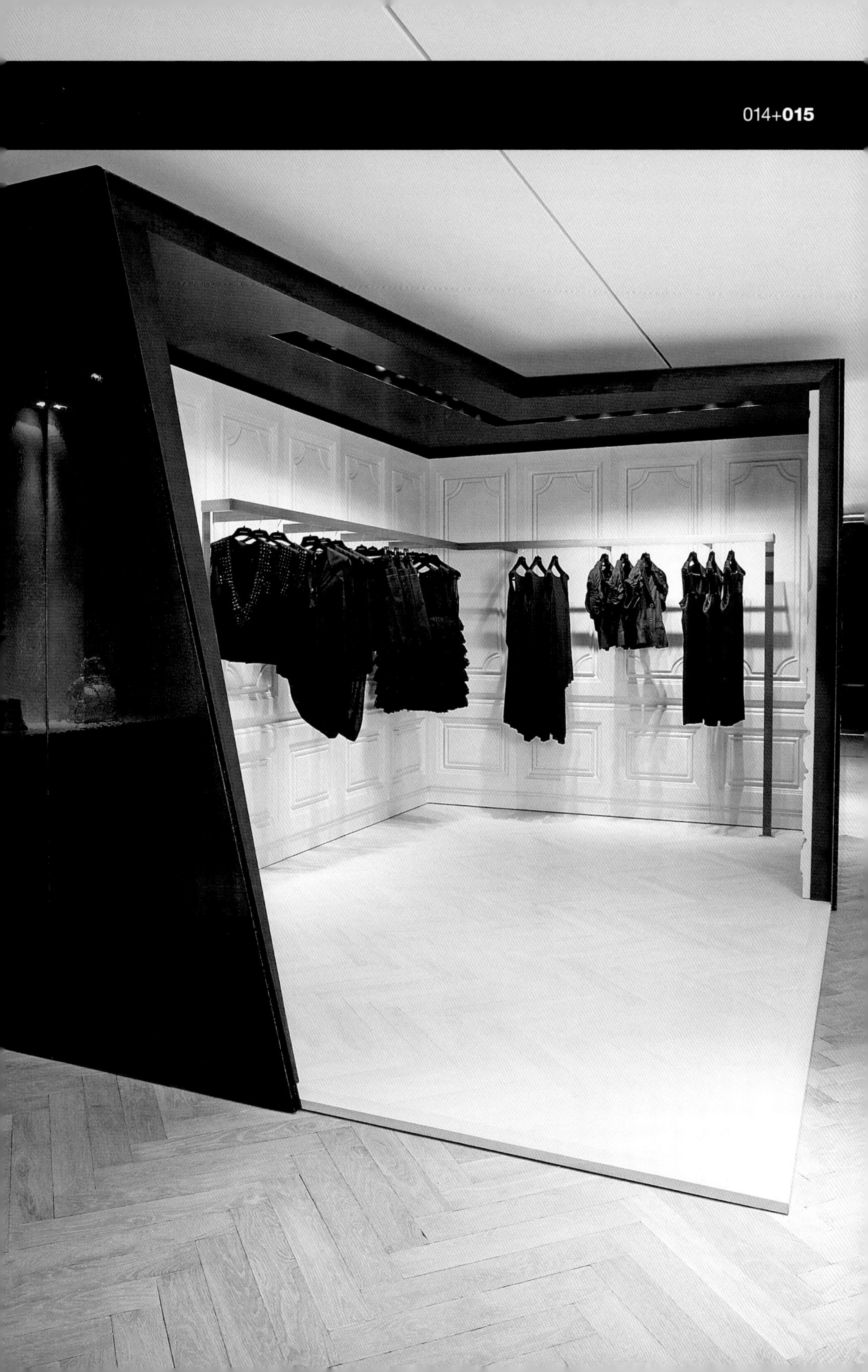

Right:
The new and the old
Stairs lead the customer up through the stack, to engage with the elaborately decorated ceiling.

Below:
The new bookshop
The over-scaled bookshelf slides through the main hall, stopping short of the café, which is situated within the apse.

Below right:
Ground floor plan
The bookshop is slipped in and around the structure of the existing building.

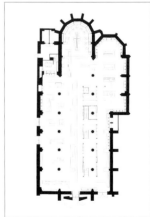

'The bookcase is a grand gesture, a statement
that matches the monumental dimensions of the church…
the object neither imposes on the space nor clashes
with the church's architecture; it enhances its experience.'

Merkx + Girod

Selexyz Dominicanen bookstore

Below:
Conceptual sketch
This brief impression illustrates
the designer's idea of the
intended insertion of the large
bookcase into the church hall.

Name:
Selexyz Dominicanen bookstore

Location:
Maastricht, Netherlands

Date:
2007

Designer:
Merkx + Girod

The dramatic location of this
bookshop demanded an equally
spectacular approach from the
designers. The store is situated
in an 800-year-old disused
Dominican church and the
designers have responded to
the sheer scale of the interior by
placing within it an element of
comparable size. Merkx + Girod
collected the many elements
of a bookshop and reassembled
them in a vast single unit.
The resulting structure, a huge
bookcase, is accommodated
within the interior of the church,
without dominating it but equally
without being overshadowed by
the scale of the existing building.

This monumental, multi-level
walk-in cabinet is placed
off-centre within the body of the
church; half of it disappears into
the side aisle, leaving a void
or space in front of the unit.
Thus, the whole elevation of the
enormous bookcase is visible
upon entering the building. The
shopper climbs into and through
the bookcase to access the
reading and display spaces on
the upper floors. This elevated
position provides the visitor
with an exceptional and unusual
view back into the building.
They are able to really appreciate
the colossal dimensions of
the church and also intimately
view the preserved historic
murals. The scheme revels in the
character of the existing building,
with the insertion of a massive
dramatic element, something
which accentuates the qualities
of both.

CaixaForum

Name:
CaixaForum

Location:
Madrid, Spain

Date:
2008

Designer:
Herzog & de Meuron

The existing building can be regarded as a distinct single object. A ruinous and disused structure can be revitalised through a radical interpretation of its exterior form.

This was the approach taken by Herzog & de Meuron at the CaixaForum cultural centre. The centre is housed in a converted 1899 brick power station. The designers placed an enormous construction on top of the original building, while simultaneously lifting the complete structure off the ground. This creates a huge, hovering and slightly unbalanced edifice, which has the incongruous qualities of being new and old, historical and contemporary, light and also heavy. A later gas station that was situated immediately in front of the building was demolished, creating a small square and thus reinforcing the theatrical qualities of the single massive element floating in space.

The removal of the base of the building allows the new plaza to flow into the museum, thus creating spaces that are neither inside nor outside; they are under the building, but are not enclosed by it. The vividness of the interior is in dramatic contrast to the decaying qualities of the exterior materials; the shiny steel, concrete and glass is as extraordinary and distinct as the bold and striking exterior. The designers have created a landmark building full of wonderful contradictions and absurdities.

Above:
The impact of the new
against the old
The textured Cor-Ten steel
contrasts strongly with
the masonry of the building.

Facing page:
View from the square
The original building is
sandwiched between
the ground level void and
the rooftop addition.

Above:
View towards the
subterranean entrance
The foyer space opens up
below the mass of the building.

Herzog & de Meuron
Jacques Herzog and Pierre de Meuron are Swiss
architects known for innovative construction, using new
materials and techniques. They revel in the exploration
of new treatments and techniques while attempting
to refine the traditions of modernism. They are continually
revolutionary and have a great capacity to shock.

There is always an intimate relationship between the existing building and the new interior, whether it is elements of an old and decaying structure or the drawn parameters of a building proposal. It may be little more than a conscious regard for the size of the space and the position of the front façade, as is prevalent in a lot of high street shop design. However, the connection could encompass many historical, contextual and structural factors, all of which can influence the quality of the space.

Above:
Museum Island
The Museum Island is situated in the middle of the river Spree, which flows through the centre of Berlin. The Neues Museum occupies a prominent position on the island.

Neues Museum

Name:
Neues Museum

Location:
Berlin, Germany

Date:
2009

Designer:
David Chipperfield Architects

The architect can take an attitude to remodelling which causes irretrievable change to the existing building, an approach that ensures that the new and the old are completely inseparable. The elements that have been placed within the existing building have become part of its nature and structure, and therefore cannot be disconnected or taken away without causing irreparable damage. This method of adaptation can be described as intervention.

Friedrich August Stueler's 1859 Neues Museum is located on the Museum Island in the heart of the former East Berlin and when it was constructed, it was considered to be the most important Prussian monument of its era. It was, until its recent remodelling, the last ruinous structure on the island – it could have been considered a picturesque classical ruin. This factor offered the architects many opportunities to manipulate the idea of history and decay. The architects developed a scheme that rationalised and made more legible the sequence of spaces through the building. This stripping out exposed and exaggerated the appearance of decay within the spaces. The museum was then populated with a series of clean, modern elements of circulation; stairs, passageways and paths that guide the visitor through the building. This strategy – intervention – uses the qualities of the existing building to generate the elements of the remodelling.

Above:
Gallery interior
The ancient qualities of the interiors were retained; the wall painting and other details were preserved in their found state and contrast strongly with the new additions.

Right:
The Grand Hall
The new main staircase is a strong and independent object within the museum. Although the language is contemporary, it feels appropriate within the space.

Below:
The exterior of the pavilion
The curving wall is an
organic form that slides within
the orthogonal structure of
the building.

'The exhibition seeks to collect and
encourage experimentation in architecture.
Such experimentation can take the
form of momentary constructions, visions
of other worlds or the building blocks
of a better world.'

Aaron Betsky

Right:
The interior of the pavilion
The undulating wall orders
and controls circulation through
the space.

Structural Oscillations

Name:
Structural Oscillations
(Swiss Pavilion at the
11th Venice Biennale)

Location:
Venice, Italy

Date:
2008 (temporary work)

Designer:
Gramazio & Kohler

A distinct and particular approach
that the designer can take to
the remodelling of an existing
building is to install a number
of freestanding elements. These
objects may be arranged in
a manner that responds to the
qualities of the host space but
does not interfere with it; the
objects do not damage or
affect the structure or finishes
of the existing. This method
of remodelling can be described
as installation.

The 11th Architecture Biennale,
entitled 'Out There: Architecture
Beyond Building', questioned
the relationship between building
and architecture. It recognised
that architecture is much more
than just keeping the rain out;
it is a way of creatively shaping
the human environment. To this
end, each exhibiting country
demonstrated the essence of their
particular architectural approach.

The Swiss Pavilion at the 2008
Venice Biennale was occupied
by an idiosyncratic undulating
element that snaked its way
through the building. The curved
brick wall was more than 100
metres in length, dividing the
space into four parts. The walls
sloped to ensure maximum
structural stability and each
enclosure or room had a different
theme. This undulating element
was in direct contrast with the
orthogonal pavilion. The curved
wall was constructed from
a material that is generally used
to build straight forms. Bricks are
normally piled vertically, one upon
another. This curved and slanting
interpretation of an orthogonal
form demonstrates contradiction
to and complexity within the
Swiss sensibility that they were
eager to represent. The exhibition
was dismantled at the end of the
Biennale and the pavilion made
ready for the next installation.

Properties of the existing site > **Methods of adaptation** > Occupation

Theatre De Trust

Name:
Theatre De Trust

Location:
Amsterdam, Netherlands

Date:
1996

Designer:
Mecanoo

The remodelling of an existing building involves a process of combining the needs of the new users with a clear understanding of the possibilities offered by the host structure. The designer can create a relationship that shows a definite separation between the new and the old, while simultaneously generating a clear connection between them. This method of adaptation can be described as insertion.

Mecanoo used this approach for the Theatre De Trust in Amsterdam. The existing building is a disused church, into which a complete and distinct object has been inserted. The two-storey church contained two empty spaces in the centre; this was originally to allow for a viewing gallery or balcony and for the (now removed) organ. The architects have positioned extremely functional elements into these voids. The first, which replaced the organ, contains ancillary activities such as the bar, kitchen, technical room and the vertical circulation. The theatre itself was inserted into the second, much larger. empty space. The residual spaces around these elements are used for gathering, meeting and circulation. The new elements slide neatly into the voids within the existing building. They are tailored objects, built to fit precisely within exact measurements of the existing building. This project utilises a strategy of insertion, which retains the integrity of the old without compromising that of the new.

Below:
The atmospheric bar
All of the services are collected together in a single element, placed in a void once occupied by the organ.

Above:
The auditorium
The raked seating was designed
to exactly fit the central void
of the building.

Right:
Conceptual model
The new service element was
designed as a single piece
of furniture built to fit exactly
within the void.

Mecanoo
Mecanoo were founded in 1984 and have developed
into one of the most significant and experimental of
Dutch practices. Their interest in unusual combinations
of materials combined with a desire to complete
buildings that are integrated with their context, creates
a design ethos with an emphasis upon architecture
that stirs the senses.

Properties of the existing site > **Methods of adaptation** > Occupation

'Occupation' describes the manner in which a space is used, inhabited and appropriated. This includes issues of habitation, enclosure, containment, organisation and function. Certain activities can occur within any sized or shaped room. Particular elements are brought together and the size, shape, colour, age, culture and nature of each of these combine to create a space that is occupied. This section will concentrate upon three interiors with the same function – a shop. However, although each space has the same use, it is occupied in a completely different way.

Facing page:
Showroom
Within the topsy-turvy interior, parquet flooring covers the ceiling and the neo-classical archway becomes a seat.

Below:
The exterior of the shop
The elements are deliberately placed upside down, projecting a contemporary attitude reflective of the designs on display inside.

Bottom:
Shop window
It is only the display of clothing that is the correct way up in this surreal interior.

Viktor & Rolf boutique

Name:
Viktor & Rolf boutique

Location:
Milan, Italy

Date:
2005

Designer:
Siebe Tettero and SZI Design

A fashion store is always more than a shop that sells clothes; it trades in image, in dreams and in aspirations. And to ensure that the customer will buy into this, the shop must project an image that the consumer wants to buy into. The fashion designers Viktor & Rolf are known for their quirky take on the classical form and they wanted their first shop to reflect this conceptual approach.

The contradiction that is inherent in their work is also evident in the design of their boutique. Everything has been turned upside down. There is oak parquet on the ceiling and chandeliers sprouting out of the floor. The fireplace, the chairs and even the TV cabinet all hang from the ceiling and the front door is obviously reversed. However, the language of the interior is clearly classical. It speaks of tradition, heritage and permanence. The detailing is exquisitely observed: the panelled walls are beautifully proportioned and the simple adapted tuscan columns and more ornate ionic pilasters are perfectly appropriate. Everything within the shop is painted a cool and subdued off-white, thus creating an atmosphere of restrained eccentricity.

The interior reflects the attitude of the designers: classic tailoring, but with an up-to-date attitude. The shop interior is occupied in a contemporary yet traditional manner.

Working with objects

Above:
The steel frame
A green steel frame raised platform denotes a display space.

Right:
Partition wall
The visual jokes, logos and slogans used in the designer's clothing ranges are reflected in the design of the shop.

Working with objects

Top:
Display elements
A garden shed is a display
element for clothes.

Above:
Counter area
The counter is a hovering beige
disc. The clothing is almost
incidental in this huge space.

Walter store

Name:
Walter store

Location:
Antwerp, Belgium

Date:
1998

Designer:
Walter Van Beirendonck

Walter, the store for the fashion
designer Walter Van Beirendonck,
has been described as part-
gallery, part-obstacle course,
part-playroom. It is situated in
a disused warehouse and is much
more than a simple boutique
to display Van Beirendonck's
ethnically inspired, flamboyant
art wear. His clothes are packed
with visual jokes, science fiction,
logos, slogans, radical statements
and cartoon characters, and
all of this is reflected in the shop.
The interior is populated with
a collection of easily identifiable
objects that have been removed
from their original context
and appropriated as elements
of display.

Half of a huge polyurethane
bear occupies a massive space
at the back of the warehouse
and conceals clothing inside it.
A great sweeping wall of plastic
bottle crates directs movement,
part of a garden shed acts as
a display unit and the counter
is a hovering beige disc. The
clothing is almost incidental in
this gallery of almost recognisable
semi-forms. The vastness and
simplicity of the warehouse
acts as a gallery space for the
exhibition of both the clothes and
the display units themselves. The
shop is occupied in a knowingly
ironic and comical manner.

Walter Van Beirendonck
Walter Van Beirendonck, was one of the so-called
'Antwerp Six', a group of designers who met
at the Antwerp Royal Academy of Fine Arts. The
group included designers who have now become
internationally recognised, such as Dries Van Noten,
Ann Demeulemeester and Dirk Bikkembergs.

Methods of adaptation > Occupation > Function

Right:
The stairwell
Elements and objects line the vertical circulation space.

Fendi showroom

Name:
Fendi showroom

Location:
Paris

Date:
2002

Designer:
Lazzarini Pickering Architetti

The Fendi showroom is a long, thin, high space. The sheer depth of the shop unit created difficulties. The shopper would not necessarily venture all the way to the back of the showroom. Lazzarini Pickering Architetti solved this by installing a collection of orthogonal objects that appear to slide through the shop. This encourages a sense of movement, both in the display cabinets and with the shopper. This three-dimensional tower acts to display the wares, while also providing the main vertical circulation route through the multi-level shop. The display cabinets themselves further reinforce the ephemeral quality. They are constructed as open boxes. These boxes seem to lack solidity; they are almost folded rectangles of pure materials. The ones at the edges of the space are constructed from dark wood, while those in the centre are made from waxed steel.

The shop is organised in a controlled yet dynamic manner. The open quality of the organisation of the shop, combined with the see-through cabinets, encourages the eye to look beyond the occupied spaces into those beyond and thus promote movement. A sense of motion exists within the shop, encouraging the visitor to explore the full depths of the space.

Working with objects

'The function of buildings in human affairs is more correctly described through patterns or rituals of occupation. Buildings will otherwise resist description in terms of more precise functions; as James Gowan has sometimes commented to me, "I can eat a sandwich in any size of room".'

Fred Scott

Below:
View through the interior
The orthogonal display elements slide through the shop.

The actual use for which an interior is designed is incredibly important. The designer needs to be able to identify the exact needs of the end-users of the interior and create appropriate spaces for their activities. The careful selection of elements to populate these places is integral to the process of combining the proposed function with the parameters of the building, while also creating the fitting image for the client. Different types of functional activity have distinct needs; for example, a shop will need different facilities to a bar or an office. It is interesting to note though, that they may not require vastly differing quality of space.

Danone Waters office

Name:
Danone Waters office

Location:
Tokyo, Japan

Date:
2005

Designer:
Klein Dytham architecture

The theme for this project was water – the product that the company collects, packages and distributes. The budget was quite small and so the designers adopted the attitude of accentuating certain areas while leaving others simple. Key areas are emphasised and these reinforce the theme, whereas the majority of the office spaces are formally organised. The open-plan office is zoned in a drifting and flowing manner. The distinct sections are defined with coloured carpeting and separated by curved, translucent screens made from suspended plastic water bottles, just like the ones sold by the company. The liquid theme is reinforced by the light fittings and the informal furniture, which are reminiscent of water droplets. In a fairly traditional open-plan office, prominence was given to particular public spaces where the nature of the business was subtly highlighted.

Above:
Workspace
The office space is divided and
controlled with a screen cleverly
constructed from water bottles.

Occupation > **Function**

The Print Room and Ink Bar

Name:
The Print Room and Ink Bar

Location:
Bournemouth, England

Date:
2006

Designer:
David Archer Architects

The Print Room draws its functional inspiration from the charm and sophistication of the continental brasserie. It combines many activities in an organised frenzy of movement and bustle. The concept was to collect a number of different but connected functional activities within a single structure. The Print Room and Ink Bar contain intimate but formal banquettes and dining booths, a more casual café area, a charcuterie, deli bar, patisserie and bakery, a private dining room, plus all the usual services such as kitchens, toilets and storerooms.

The original building was the print room of the local newspaper, the *Daily Echo*, hence the name. This beautiful art deco construction provided the stylistic influence for the design of the new interior. The streamlined and angular qualities of the retained exterior were transported into the interior. This contained space was huge, some 370 square metres, with a seven-metre-high ceiling level. The designer divided this vast room in an orthogonal manner to accommodate the different activities. This could have been chaotic, but the organisational concept was reinforced by a chequered floor finish, which reflected the art deco influence and unified the room.

The collection of related but different functions was drawn together in a single space. Each area was integrated into the whole through the use of a common design language. The strict organisation ensured that each area was autonomous, while still belonging to the same family.

Facing page:
The Charcuterie and Ink Bar
The space is organised in a very orthogonal manner, reinforced by the chequered floor pattern.

Top:
Exterior of the brasserie
The art deco façade influenced the design of the interior.

Above:
The private dining room
The table was specifically designed to occupy this room. It is a contemporary interpretation of an art deco object. Note how the chequered floor also continues into this space.

Ergonomics
Ergonomics is the science of the relationship between people and their immediate environment. It is the study of how objects can best be designed for comfort, safety, efficiency and productivity.

Occupation > Function

Facing page:
The dance floor and the bar
The interior is populated with
a collage of industrial elements.

Right:
The view through the foyer
The clubber emerges from
the dark and dismal foyer area,
through the portal, and into the
cavernous expanse of the club.

The Haçienda

Name:
The Haçienda

Location:
Manchester, England

Date:
1982

Designer:
Ben Kelly Design (BKD)

A specific object can be loaded
with significance and meaning.
The arch is a threshold, a
transition point; it is the position
in which a person passes from
one condition into the next. It is
the place that the visitor prepares
for the spatial event to come.

This is the approach the Ben Kelly
Design took to the design of the
now demolished Haçienda Club
in Manchester. This contemporary
postmodern interpretation
of an arch is a single element
in a series of objects that guides
the club-goer from the almost
anonymous entrance into the
writhing heart of the club. This
is a very dramatic architectural
promenade that directs the visitor
through a number of different
experiences and spaces. The
journey always began outside,
in the queue, then eventually
through the cramped ticket office,
past the dark and miserable
cloakroom, between the plastic
curtain and then finally through
the arch, when the full and
massive industrial glory of the
club was revealed.

The arch itself was very simple,
a pigeon-blue freestanding
square block with a rectangular
chunk asymmetrically removed
from it. The arch was positioned
diagonally across the threshold,
which acted to only partially
reveal the space beyond and thus
suspend, just for a second, the
impact of the warehouse space.

Promenade
Architectural promenade is a device that allows space
to be seen moving rather than as static. It encourages
the viewer to continually reassess their relationship with
the building. The designer will arrange the rooms, spaces,
views and sightlines to open up for the user as they
move (or promenade) through the space.

Occupation > Function

The new interior will offer an assemblage of different restrictions and opportunities. The drawn parameters of a building proposal will contain a series of conditions which, when combined with the functional needs of the users, will form the basis of the design. This will often offer the chance for the designer to work directly with the architect to develop the qualities of the interior space. The manner in which the elements and objects occupy the space is a negotiation between the designer, the architect, the client and the user.

Name:
Seattle Public Library
(see pp 056+057)

Location:
Seattle, USA

Date:
2004

Designer:
OMA and LMN Architects

Methods of organisation

Purposely positioned objects can manipulate the manner in which an interior is perceived. The designer of a new interior has the opportunity to work closely with the architect on the production of a space that is suitable, practicable and agreeable. The arrangement of the elements and forms that occupy the interior can be based upon the most amenable agreement rather than upon the limitations of an existing structure. Normally there are still certain restrictions, such as the position of the structure and other contextual considerations, but these can be seen as points of liberation.

Form

The actual size and shape of the elements of occupation (which is the form of the individual objects within an interior), is a crucial and expressive decision for the designer. The elements can blend with the space, in that they can reinforce the idea that underpins the design. Conversely, the object can act as a foil or counterbalance to the main design theme; it can, perhaps, stand out as an organic shape among a crowd of orthogonal forms.

Scale is an important consideration, and furniture usually expresses human scale; it is designed ergonomically to fit the body. Furniture that is larger or smaller can look incongruous and out of place. This may be a deliberate tactic; for example, children's furniture is appropriately child-sized, while a throne is always over-scaled. Scale allows comparisons to be made; the placement of a much bigger object in a field of smaller ones invites contrast and juxtaposition.

Materials

The surface finish of an object can have a direct influence upon the attitude towards it; for example, a chair that is covered with leather is viewed differently to one finished with fun-fur, which is different again to canvas, silk or even rubber. The manner in which the materials are held together also influences the perception of it. Contemporary minimalism has encouraged designers to create pure forms and reduce the detail around junction and joints to almost nothing. The Victorians enjoyed celebrating this meeting of materials and used embellished detail in these positions.

Function

The designer of the new interior has an opportunity to create a space that is perfectly suited to its function. The needs of the end-users obviously have an enormous influence upon the organisation, the form and the surface finishes of the design elements. The functional requirements of those who will occupy the interior are an important contributing factor in the collection of design generators and ultimately upon the nature and the quality of the space.

Facing page:
The Collection, Lincoln, England
(see pp 046+047).

Unlike many other creative businesses, such as graphic, industrial or fashion design, the interior designer always has to respond to a given environment: the building within which the interior is situated. With new interiors, this may be little more than the drawn parameters of a building proposal; this still offers many opportunities and restrictions. The size and shape of a building are given, as are many contextual issues such as the relationship with the street, the sun and nearby buildings, and other physical features. There may also be internal elements, such as the stairs and lift, the structure, columns, beams, walls and the position of the doors and windows. The designer must be aware of all these constraints when considering the organisation of the new interior.

Top:
Exterior view of the building
The curtain wall glazing allows the maximum penetration of natural light into the building.

Above:
Ground floor foyer
The barrier-like concrete structural wall controls and regulates the amount of light admitted into the interior space.

Objects in the new interior

Right:
The gallery
Natural light is allowed to enter the service areas surrounding the gallery space. This is then bounced and filtered across the ceilings of the internal galleries, thus controlling the amount of light that reaches the art works.

Bregenz Art Gallery

Name:
Bregenz Art Gallery

Location:
Bregenz, Austria

Date:
1997

Designer:
Peter Zumthor

The Bregenz Art Gallery is located in the most spectacular setting on the edge of Lake Constance. It is a dramatic and austere statement in a mountainous and leafy environment. The building is separated from the lake by a series of transport networks: the harbour, a railway track and a main road. It is therefore positioned some distance from the shore and can consequently be easily distinguished from the general jumble of other buildings.

The art gallery is clad with curtain wall glazing; this allows the maximum amount of natural light to enter the building, as initially there are no barriers to its ingress. However, the method of internal organisation dictates how that natural light is admitted into the gallery spaces. This manner of control is made apparent by its own silhouette on the glass of the exterior cladding. A concrete structure acts to support the building and to obscure and manage the entry of natural light and control the internal organisation. The building is organised in a very straightforward manner. The square galleries are at the centre of each floor. These are separated from the exterior walls by a surrounding layer of service areas, such as circulation, toilets and ducts.

Natural light within a gallery is both useful and dangerous. It is useful, because to appreciate anything visual, the viewer needs to be able to see it and natural light is both abundant and cheap. It also provides a direct connection with the exterior environment; the changing nature of it can tie an interior space to the outside world. It is dangerous because its intensity can damage and cause decay to delicate works of art. The designer appreciated these inherent contradictions and embraced the qualities that natural light can give to an inside room. He designed the building to allow all the natural light that enters through the glass walls to be bounced and filtered through the circulation areas and across the ceilings of the internal galleries. Inevitably this light is not constant, unlike artificial light, which is always of the same intensity. However, it does allow the visitor to continually reconnect, in a tenuous and abstract manner, with the beautiful and extraordinary external setting.

Introduction > **Methods of organisation** > Form

Objects in the new interior

Above:
The central area
The raised through route circulates above the open museum courtyard.

Left:
The urban promenade
The public route through the building snakes around the open courtyard.

'In the enclosed garden a polarity emerges; the paradox of the infinite in the finite, two extremes heightened by being present simultaneously.'

Rob Aben and Saskia de Wit

Neue Staatsgalerie

Name:
Neue Staatsgalerie

Location:
Stuttgart, Germany

Date:
1984

Designer:
James Stirling

A courtyard is an odd place; it is neither inside nor outside. It is within the parameters of the site, the walls of the building enclose it, but it is outside, it is an exterior element. The courtyard is often a haven of peace and quiet, a place of order and pleasure in a chaotic and hostile world. This enclosed and protected space can be observed throughout the history of architecture. It can be seen from early mediaeval monasteries to Moorish palaces in Granada. The courtyard provided quiet relief from the hectic atmosphere of the urban environment, and protection from potentially unfriendly and unsympathetic intruders.

The courtyard, or enclosed garden, still has a place within design at the beginning of the twenty-first century. This is especially relevant within domestic design; urban space is ever more limited and a quiet outside refuge is a valuable and often vital resource. The courtyard can also make a dramatic architectural statement, particularly within a public building. For example, it presents the art gallery with the opportunity to engage with the exterior world without the need for the visitor to actually leave the premises. This inside/outside space is ideal for a moment of relaxation during the intense journey through the succession of interiors-focussed gallery rooms.

James Stirling placed a huge circular courtyard at the centre of the Staatsgalerie in Stuttgart. This enormous element acts at ground level, as a point of intellectual escape for the gallery visitors. They can remove themselves from the concentration of the interior spaces and enter this protective and enclosed space that has an open roof to the sky. At high level, this courtyard also acts as a through-route. The path around the edge of the drum allows pedestrians to pass through the gallery, without actually entering the building. The style is classical; it is clad in horizontal stripes of sandstone, with exposed joints and enlarged details. It is the postmodern interpretation of the ancient Roman forum.

Right:
The courtyard
The robust exterior is finished
in local Lincolnshire limestone.

Facing page:
The restaurant
The public areas occupy the
open spaces between the blocks.

The Collection museum

Name:
The Collection museum

Location:
Lincoln, England

Date:
2005

Designer:
Panter Hudspith Architects

The designer has the opportunity
to respond to the particular
context of a building. Panter
Hudspith Architects envisioned
this museum as a collection
of huge blocks or elements
that almost appear to tumble
down the hill in this historic
urban environment. Lincoln is
a town of two distinct parts: the
spectacular historic cathedral
occupies the top of a steep hill,
above old and winding streets
that lead down to the mundane
modern town centre.

The museum is situated
between these two elements
and attempts to pull them
together. The building is a direct
response to the character and
scale of medieval Lincoln. It was
conceived as a group of buildings
rather than a single structure.
It was envisaged as five blocks
of stone, with the public spaces
in the gaps between them.
The largest space creates
a public square and this is linked
to the other gaps, which form
a passageway into the heart
of the museum. These interior/
exterior spaces are finished
in local Lincolnshire limestone,
with timber and bronze detailing.
This gives the spaces a strong
and robust character. Light enters
the rooms from above and filters
across the rough, riven surfaces
of the block buildings, reinforcing
the exterior quality.

The public interior spaces were
created from the spaces between
the blocks of museum building.
The materials used would
normally be found on the exterior
of a building and the lighting is
predominately natural. The rough
and uncompromising quality
of the finishes reinforces the
exterior character of these
internal spaces. But the spaces
are enclosed; they are warm,
dry and conditioned. These
interior spaces are reminiscent
of the small enclosed streets
of the old town.

'Our movements are ever subject to the same physical forces as are built forms and may be physically contained, limited and directed by these forms.'

Kent C Bloomer
Charles W Moore
Robert J Yudell

The carefully designed element can be a dramatic form within an interior. The designer can accentuate a particular object so that it becomes the focus of the space. The other elements of the design may be less expressive; thus, the contrast between them and the feature element would be made more extreme. The designer can deliberately ensure that the shape and size of the special object communicates the function or use, or else forms a more abstract sculptural focal point within the space.

Konditor & Cook shop and café

Name:
Konditor & Cook shop and café

Location:
London, England

Date:
2007

Designer:
Jamie Fobert Architects

A designer may wish to deliberately contrast a sculptural form of an interior element with the form of a building. This will serve to both advertise and distinguish the particular interior from the rest of the building. 30 St Mary Axe (formerly known as the Swiss Re Tower) by Foster + Partners is an iconic and highly recognisable building on the London skyline. Its extraordinary shape has earned it the nickname of the Gherkin. Jamie Fobert Architects were commissioned to install a cake shop on the ground floor of this landmark.

The designers were determined not to emulate the language of the original architects and took the approach of designing an interior that obviously fits into the space, but is not joined to it. A huge steel mezzanine simply hangs in the double height room; it is suspended from the ceiling and floats above the main café area. This upper level is a private area that contains the kitchen and other workspaces and the visitor views it as a floating sculptural form. The materials of the cake shop also stand out from the building; black and coloured glass and black steel. Full-height windows throw natural light into the depths of the space and illuminate the substantial forms of the mezzanine and the counter. The cakes are warm jewels in among this massive and brutal interior.

The designers have constructed an interior that is not intimidated by the immensity of the building; instead they have used the qualities of the materials, the scale and the light to create a dramatic and distinctive space.

Above:
View towards the mezzanine
The preparation area hovers
above the café area.

Right:
First floor plan
The balcony occupies most
of this double-height space.

Far right:
Ground floor plan
The space is free to allow for
movement and interaction.

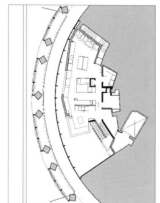

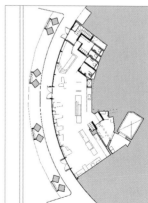

Above:
View toward arcoseleum
The sarcophogi nestle beneath
their shelter.

Left:
The Brion Tomb
The architect exploits the
organic nature of the site.

'I wanted to render the natural sense of the concept of water and field, water and life: water is the source of life.'

Carlo Scarpa

Brion Monumental Tomb

Name:
Brion Monumental Tomb

Location:
San Vito d'Altivole, Italy

Date:
1978

Designer:
Carlo Scarpa

A particular object can become the focus of a design, it can be the point to which everything else defers. The language of all the objects may be similar, but the manner of the organisation will highlight the most important element within the collection. It may encourage the visitor or user to concentrate upon something specific.

The Brion cemetery is much more than a repository or grave, it is a landscape dedicated to the life of a single person. It is the antithesis of the stacked or closely packed burial chambers normally found in Italy. Within this landscape is a collection of elements, all of which contribute towards this celebration.

The actual sarcophagus is a modest and fairly unobtrusive element within the design. It is placed, with its partner, directly upon the ground, deliberately close to the earth. An unadorned reinforced concrete arch protects the tombs. These incredibly simple forms are very powerful; the lack of complexity, combined with the direct connection with the earth lends a reverence to the pieces. Also present within the openness of the walled garden are a small chapel and a floating island of contemplation. This beautiful combination of devotion and reflection allows the focus to be placed upon austere and seemingly effortless forms.

Above:
The chapel
The chapel appears to float ethereally upon the water.

Methods of organisation > **Form** > Materials

'In the fertile streets and market places of town and village it is the focal point (be it column or cross) which crystallises the situation, which confirms "this is the spot".'

Gordon Cullen

Eden Court Theatre

Name:
Eden Court Theatre

Location:
Inverness, Scotland

Date:
2007

Designer:
Page \ Park Architects
with Donald Urquhart

There are certain elements within the design of a building that the architect or designer is obliged to accommodate. Most buildings must contain fire exits, circulation, lifts, ducts, toilets and ventilation. These are often parts of the building that are deliberately played down; emphasis is placed on what could be considered as more important areas of the building. However, this is not the approach that Page \ Park Architects took to the remodelling of the Eden Court Theatre. They worked with an artist, Donald Urquhart, to draw attention to the ventilation towers.

Law and Dunbar Naismith originally designed the Eden Court Theatre in 1976, next to the 1878 Bishop's Palace. It has been substantially redeveloped to provide an additional theatre, two cinemas, two studios and office accommodation. The new facilities wrap around the existing building, exploiting the original foyer skirt and then stepping down to allow the formation of a café terrace overlooking the river and landscaped grounds. This is all assembled under a simple roof, extending forward to provide cover to the external seating terrace. This creates an appropriate civic presence to the riverfront and to the city beyond. The asymmetry of the new extension and the design of the tall ventilation towers echo the form of Bishop's Palace.

The new spaces are naturally ventilated; this has had a great influence over the architecture of the new extension. The six large ventilation towers have been boldly clad in black, blue and polished stainless steel to a design by artist Donald Urquhart. This collaboration between the architects and the artist has created elements that have a dramatic sculptural quality; these are objects that are often designed to be deliberately anonymous, to blend in with the background. But this relationship has highlighted and placed focus upon these extraordinary objects.

Right:
The foyer
The foyer is a dramatic and useful space.

Top:
View from the street
The sculptural chimney is a focal
point at the front of the building.

Above:
New meets old
The original building is in balance
with the new extension.

The specific choice of materials and textures can give identity and meaning to an element. For example, the character of a wall depends as much upon its textural quality as it does its structure or position. A coarse, rough concrete finish has a quite different quality to that of polished marble and different again to studded rubber or fun fur, even though they can all quite viably be placed in an identical position. The application of a wide variety of surface materials, some drawn from unorthodox sources, can create an unusual identity. Materials such as steel mesh, plastics and acrylic, which were developed for industrial use, are now widely accepted as interior finishes. This crossover of use can create an odd yet often appropriate atmosphere and mood in an interior space.

Below:
Reception
This painted screen provides a backdrop to the desk and conceals storage .

Wallraf-Richartz Museum shop

Name:
Wallraf-Richartz Museum shop

Location:
Cologne, Germany

Date:
2001

Designer:
O.M. Ungers

O.M. Ungers was well known for the rigorous grid that informed his buildings. This sense of control extended through the planning, structure and cladding, all the way to the organisation of the interior. The Wallraf-Richartz Museum shop is situated in the foyer of the museum and is controlled in the same meticulous manner as the rest of the building. The display cabinets are carefully positioned with the boundary of the square grid and the proportions reflect the scale of the building. However, the materials that cover the containing and controlling walls are much softer than the granite, concrete and glass used elsewhere.

These dividing barriers have been covered with fabric, in strong contrast to the rest of the museum. This fabric has been detailed in the same rigorous way as the building. It is divided into a grid of metre squares, which exactly correspond to the ceiling grid.

The other screen walls within the foyer have been treated with equal thoroughness. The coloured wall that is situated behind the reception desk is deep red and the screen that separates the shop from the foyer is magenta. It has a long, horizontal back-lit display cabinet set into it. The design of the interior and the elements within it reflects and heightens the precise and controlling grid that dominates the building.

Left:
The padded wall
This wall acts as a barrier between the gallery shop and exhibition area.

Below left:
The fuschia wall
This wall acts as a barrier that contains the foyer space and also serves to display exhibition items.

'Blaisse, the Dutch designer of interiors and landscapes and known for her striking collaborations with Rem Koolhaas, has a talent for turning nature into culture and culture into nature. She is in a sense, architecture's experimental earth mother, convincing builders of glass, cement and steel monuments to pay attention to – of all things – curtains and gardens.'

Melissa Milgrom

Seattle Public Library

Name:
Seattle Public Library

Location:
Seattle, USA

Date:
2004

Designer:
OMA and LMN Architects

Facing page:
The open space of the library
Huge graphic carpets delineate areas of the library, such as bookshelves and reading spaces.

Below:
Conceptual diagram
The 'library stack' of soft furnishings.

The Seattle Public Library is a radical building; it asks the question: what, at the beginning of the twenty-first century, is a library for? It attempts to address this question, to accept the technological innovations that have changed how a library is used and to recognise the changes in attitude towards such a building.

The building was conceived rather like a huge, open warehouse, in which individual areas are defined not by walls and rooms, but through the use of ornament and texture. Soft furnishings – the carpet and the curtains – are employed at an architectural scale. The curtains are double or even triple height and are used to delineate and enclose particular spaces. When they are open, the spaces flow into one another; when closed they contain a room, acting not only to exclude the light, but also to muffle the sound and control movement. Carpets demarcate the limitation of particular activities; within the huge and open-plan building, they fix specific functions in a definite area.

The carpets and the curtains were custom designed by Petra Blaisse of Inside Outside. The carpet was made by Ege from aquafil face yarn. The curtains, however, are of more traditional materials, such as velvet and canvas. Petra Blaisse has created a series of dramatic statements in an extraordinary setting.

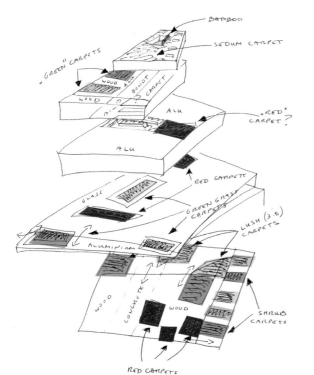

Aquafil face yarn
Aquafil face yarn, a recycled product, is a nylon or polyamid yarn, which is a non-absorbable monofilament or braided synthetic material.

Form > Materials > Function

Above:
The pavilion in the park
The organic temporary structure flowed from the landscape in which it was situated.

Right:
The café
The random scattering of chairs reinforced the temporary nature of the structure.

'The Serpentine Pavilion each year gives the opportunity for a small structure to be built without the demands of a complex brief – allowing the chance to experiment and the pushing of boundaries.'

Cecil Balmond

Serpentine Gallery Pavilion

Name:
Serpentine Gallery Pavilion

Location:
London, England

Date:
2005 (temporary work)

Designer:
Álvaro Siza and
Eduardo Souto de Moura with
Cecil Balmond

The Serpentine Pavilion presented the opportunity for the designers to create a small temporary structure, without the constraints of a more permanent building. The design of a pavilion, whether it is inside a great trade exhibition hall, or an artful one-off, is a particular and creative prospect. The normal limitations that accompany a more long-lasting project do not apply. Usually the client wishes for some sort of expressive statement; therefore ephemeral materials and techniques can be experimented with, and innovative shapes and forms can be tested.

The organic Serpentine Pavilion was designed to flow from the parkland within which it was situated. It was intended to appear as a natural element among a collection of rural elements. The roof and the walls were made out of a corrugated grid of laminated wood and the structure comprised 427 wooden beams joined together using mortise-and-tenon joints. The roof was covered with 248 polycarbonate panels. This created a flowing structure that was 17 metres wide at its widest point. The pavilion, which was open at the sides, was populated with randomly arranged chairs, tables and a serving unit. This organisation reinforced the ephemeral quality of the structure.

The pavilion was a large experimental object, borne from contemporary design combined with contextual integration; the materials used in its construction reflected this interest in technical innovation mixed with tradition.

Above:
Detail of the structure
The laminated wood structure was covered in a series of polycarbonate panels. These were missing at the corners of the building to allow for circulation and to let the view in and out of the pavilion.

Form > **Materials** > Function

The designer sometimes has the opportunity to explicitly express the functional use of the building within the organisation of the interior. This can be achieved in a variety of ways, but the most obvious is through the use of objects that have a direct relationship with the function. These may be period pieces or actual working examples, but the intention is to unequivocally represent the purpose of the space. Another approach is for the designer to abstract the idea, so that the use is signalled in a more subtle and conceptual manner. There are certain ideas within society that can be expressed through the use of cultural symbols, and this is another method of communication that the designer can exploit.

Facing page:
The tasting bar
The slate counter has a conceptual crack of gold running through it; this symbolises both the locality and values of the brand.

Below:
Reception area
A wall of barrels robustly separates the different spaces of the interior.

Objects in the new interior

Penderyn Distillery

Name:
Penderyn Distillery

Location:
Brecon Beacons, Wales

Date:
2008

Designer:
David Archer Architects

The Penderyn Distillery is the only whisky distillery in Wales and one of the smallest distilleries in the world. It is located high in the Brecon Beacons, on a spring of natural mineral water in an area of outstanding natural beauty.

David Archer Architects have explicitly used the mechanical distilling process as a backdrop for the design of the reception and tasting area. Twenty or so of the sherry-soaked casks, which are used to store the whisky in while it ages, are used as room dividers. These barrels not only visually signal the process but also give off a rich odour of whisky, sherry and wood. The reception area also offers views directly into the still, bottling area and cooperage store, again creating a direct connection with the functional process of the factory.

Another more subtle connection with the product is decoratively explored on the tasting bar. The whisky bottle labels are black, with an embossed gold seam; this represents the purity and value of the water as it runs through the slate that is so bountiful in the area. This black and gold motif has been reproduced on the counter. This dramatic element is actually constructed from huge pieces of slate, set into which is a seam of brightly polished brass. This vein of gold runs up the face of the counter and across the top.

The designers have reinforced the functional use of the interior space through a series of well thought-out and strategically positioned elements.

Materials > **Function**

Above:
View through the
circulation space
Roof lights illuminate the central
passage. Bookshelves are used
to control and arrange the space.

'Interior architecture seeks to combine the positive attributes of both the architect and the interior designer to achieve holistically complete interior space.'

John Kurtich and Garret Eakin

Deisgner's residence

Name:
Designer's residence

Location:
Toronto, Canada

Date:
2005

Designer:
John L. Johnson

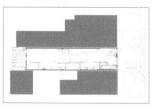

Top:
Axonometric
The long thin interior is populated by a series of coordinated elements.

Above:
Plan
The centre of the space is left deliberately open to facilitate circulation.

An interior can be populated with a collection of useful and functional objects, which can be used in a creative manner. The designer can generate forms that can direct and organise the space as well as behave functionally. For example, a wall can be much more than a simple white vertical surface. Book shelving can divide space and act as a backdrop for many different activities. Fitted furniture, such as counters and storage units, does not need to be positioned against party walls, it can be placed in the heart of the space, thus providing a point of focal interest and encouraging people to partake in the functional activity.

John L. Johnson took this approach for the design of his own house in Toronto. The house, situated in an old factory, is a long and thin space, with natural light entering only from the short sides or from above. The designer has not cluttered the room with dividing walls; instead, furniture is used to control and arrange the specific areas of the interior. The kitchen counter, which protrudes into the space, is positioned under a top light. It is placed at the centre of the space and acts as a fulcrum around which everything rotates. The overcrowded bookshelves line the space, which encourages the eye to traverse the length of the room and the dining table is placed in a quiet, sunny area at the end of the room. As this is a piece of fixed furniture, access to the door is always maintained.

The designer has used functional pieces of furniture to change what is an awkwardly shaped room into an engaging interior full of incident and occasion.

Materials > **Function**

Right:
Library exterior
The building is situated on a raised plinth.

Museum of Modern Literature

Name:
Museum of Modern Literature

Location:
Marbach am Neckar, Germany

Date:
2007

Designer:
David Chipperfield Architects

A colonnade is an element that serves many functions within a building. It is basically a row of columns joined by an entablature or by arches. If it is positioned at the entrance of a building, it is a portico, and if it encloses the passage around a courtyard, it is a cloister. It can act protectively, by providing shelter from the weather for the users of the building, whether this is shade from the sun or refuge from the rain. A colonnade can also signal the type of building; it is an authoritarian element and can indicate a sense of purpose, wisdom and learning. Consequently, they are traditionally found in front of art galleries and other public buildings. A colonnade does not enclose rooms, it usually contains points of change or circulation.

The colonnade around the Museum of Modern Literature is severe and minimal. It signals the merit and value of the building and it expresses the very serious nature of the contents. It also acts to screen and protect the building. The gallery spaces are at the lower level, so this protruding box contains the reception area, foyer and space for temporary exhibitions. The colonnade prevents the ingress of excessive solar gain, which is always a problem with a glazed building. It is also a canopy, under which the visitors can shelter before and after their gallery tour. The colonnade is not placed symmetrically around the entrance area box; it protrudes further at the southern side, thus providing greater shade where necessary.

In 2007, the architects won the RIBA Stirling Prize for this dramatic and not uncontroversial statement of a building.

'A clearly defined material concept using solid materials (fair-faced concrete, sandblasted reconstituted stone with limestone aggregate, limestone, wood, felt and glass) gives the calm, rational architectural language a sensual physical presence.'

World Architecture News

Above:
The colonnade
The colonnade acts to screen the building from sunlight.

Left:
The reading room
The visitor can take books from within the controlled depths of the museum and move into this daylit room to read them.

Below left:
Exhibition space
The fragile works of literature are sensitively protected within the carefully illuminated heart of the building.

The design and positioning of particular objects
and elements that inhabit the existing building
is a process of exploring and taking advantage
of the opportunities and constraints inherent within
the original structure. The new elements do not have
to merge in with the old, they do not have to match
or blend in. An examination of the already-built will
offer many occasions to create contrast, counterpoint
and distinction. A pristine object can make a very
dramatic statement when situated within a decaying
interior. This unique quality can be further enhanced
if the contemporary form is built to fit exactly within
the ancient host building. This act of creating
bespoke furniture, of whatever size, adds aesthetic
value to the interior, the building and the new
elements within.

Name:
Magna Science Adventure Centre
(see pp 084+085)

Location:
Rotherham, England

Date:
2001

Designer:
Wilkinson Eyre Architects

Methods of organisation

The existing building offers many opportunities; it may have old or even ancient qualities that can be exposed and exploited. This is often desirable, it proffers an image of trusted permanence and continuity; it is a link with the past. However, it can also act as a constraint, especially if the building is listed. The amount of changes that the designer can make to the structure is often limited and the shape and nature of the possible spaces has to be studied carefully. This can encourage the designer to think in a more ephemeral manner. Possible directions include temporary installations that do not interfere with the original building; constructing gleaming insertions that contrast with a dull and decaying interior and using freestanding elements that do not touch the walls of the interior to organise the space.

Form

The form of the old has a direct influence over the form of the new. The designer will interpret the existing to create the new. The original building will have a distinct and unique size and shape and it is the analysis and elucidation of this that encourages the designer to create elements and objects that are appropriate to their surroundings. This does not mean pastiche, or copying the style, it is much more of an interpretation. The contrast and difference of new elements against the old interior can create spaces of distinction.

Materials

The attitude that the designer takes towards the choice of materials is a very important contributor to the quality of the space. The designer can select materials and details that are totally in keeping with the age of the building. This approach could almost be seen as restoration because the new and the old are hardly distinguishable. Conversely, the designer may select materials of extreme contrast to the existing structure. This would create spaces that exhibit counterbalance and distinction, but providing that there is a sense of equilibrium within the interior, it can be a very effective approach. A third method is for the designer to use materials that are sympathetic to the old, but are designed and detailed in a contemporary or modern fashion. This approach distinguishes between the new and the old, but can create spaces that exhibit a sense of continuity.

Function

If a building is remodelled, the original purpose for which the building was constructed is usually different to the new function. The needs and the expectations of the users are not the same. An ancient building, or perhaps even one that was constructed in the twentieth century, does not generally contain the facilities necessary for twenty-first century use. Therefore, the designer must understand the functional requirements of those who are to occupy the remodelled building, and combine this knowledge with a thorough understanding of the qualities of the existing spaces.

Above:
Haus im Haus, Hamburg,
Germany (see pp 076+077).

Carefully placed objects can control the manner in which space is occupied. They can control movement and circulation and delineate areas that are to be used for particular activities, while also influencing the occupier's expectations of the space. An interior that is overflowing with soft furnishings will be used in a different way to one that is austere and minimal. The user has distinct expectations of different types of materials; he or she will act in a particular manner depending upon the robustness, fragility, warmth, preciousness or other specific quality exuded by the materials that make up the space.

Below:
Bookcase closed
The freestanding, multifunctional element divides and controls the interior.

Objects in the existing building

Right:
Bookcase open
The purity of the sculptural
element allows the
focus to be placed upon
the sculptural furniture.

Allmeinde Commongrounds

Name:
Allmeinde Commongrounds

Location:
Lech am Arlberg, Austria

Date:
2006

Designer:
Katia Polletin and
Gerold Schneider

A single adaptable element can provide for the majority of the functional services within an interior. This gathering together of all the practical and service activities will leave the rest of the space relatively empty. This will allow the character of the interior to become apparent and any freestanding furniture to be points of focal interest.

This is the approach taken by Katia Polletin and Gerold Schneider in their conversion of a barn into an informal forum for arts, architecture and discussion. 'Allmeinde' literally means 'common ground', or that communal open area that is cooperatively utilised by all members of a local community. Artists, theorists and authors are invited to spend time in this multicultural centre in order to study in depth the past and present and to contribute to the future of the Alpine culture.

The ground floor of the conversion is book-lined and contains the meeting room, with a table that seems to extend through the large picture window into the Alpine slopes beyond. However, it is the first floor that contains a more dramatic statement. A huge, horizontal wooden bookcase-type element occupies the complete length of the space. It is placed off centre and initially appears to act as hanging or exhibition space. It soon becomes apparent that this element is much more versatile than that. Full-height doors within the unit open to reveal the useful service areas. A desk folds from the centre, a small kitchen unfolds from the end and even a bed opens out from this wonderful and adaptable freestanding unit. The sparse interior is populated with primitive wooden furniture and the complete installation is totally appropriate to its location in the tree-lined mountains of southern Austria.

Introduction > Methods of organisation > Form

'[Scarpa] insists that architecture must embrace "uneasiness" and "anxiety"… moments of incompleteness and disquieting unfamiliarity.'

Nicholas Olsberg

Castelvecchio Museum

Name:
Castelvecchio Museum

Location:
Verona Italy

Date:
1964

Designer:
Carlo Scarpa

Objects within museums and galleries do not have to be displayed in an obvious and regular manner: a more fluid or sensitive approach can create spaces of great character. Within the Castelvecchio Museum, object and movement are inseparable. In his remodelling of the building, Scarpa used one to reinforce the other. The paintings and sculptures are used to orientate and direct movement and view. Objects are used to illustrate narrative breaks in the building's history, their placement often emphasising an important junction. Visitors are encouraged to move in an organic manner through the series of spaces, to concentrate upon an object and then move to the next in an unconscious yet highly organised way.

The Castelvecchio Museum in Verona is a complex of buildings, courtyards, gardens and a tower of the Scaliger Castle. It is situated by a bridge over the river Adige, which runs through the centre of Verona. The bridge marks the line of the old wall that surrounded the city and divided the castle in two; on the eastern city side was the fortified garrison and on the other the residential palace.

The museum was designed to house a collection of sculptures, paintings and artefacts dedicated to the city and the surrounding area from the twelfth to the eighteenth centuries. Within the main gallery spaces, the sculptures, ornaments and other objects are positioned so that they prevent the visitor from promenading directly through the rooms. The objets d'art are in the way. They are placed upon pedestals, carefully positioned to take advantage of the natural light and are therefore displayed in a dramatic and atmospheric manner; shade is as important as light. The sculptures punctuate the space, they become visual events in the journey through the gallery.

Above:
View through the ground floor galleries
Each artefact is placed upon a plinth, which gives the appearance of floating or hovering above the floor.

Facing page:
Interior of the ground floor gallery
The natural light is deliberately controlled as it enters the room and illuminates the meticulously positioned sculptures.

'The banqueting table is internationally recognised as a space where acquaintances are made, plans forged and deals done. We were interested in the idea of conversations rising and falling along the table – across the table, in groups, side by side.'

Roger Mann

Above:
Atmospheric lighting
Ever-changing theatrical lighting lent a sense of drama to the installation.

Facing page:
The long table
This display exploits the social etiquette of a formal dining situation.

'Great Expectations' exhibition

Name:
'Great Expectations' exhibition

Location:
New York, USA

Date:
2001 (temporary work)

Designer:
Casson Mann

Exhibition design allows designers to create ephemeral installations. These are interiors that are not expected to have an infinite life but to last for a fixed period of time. 'Great Expectations', an exhibition designed to promote British products and services, was a reaction to the frenzy of modern life. Casson Mann's brief was to create an eye-catching and exciting exhibition design that would showcase the best of contemporary British design to the thousands of travellers passing daily through Grand Central Station. Since it was likely that many of these would be in a hurry, the design had to be dramatic, playful and easily accessible.

The designers created an illuminated 50-metre-long banqueting table, which glowed brilliant white and was covered with a dramatic display of objects. The hurried commuters encountered a very different space from the one they were used to, and the visitors could choose to engage with the piece through just looking or actually sitting down and consequently becoming part of the installation. A banqueting table immediately evokes the idea of dialogue and interaction; it is designed to encourage convivial conversation and thus to represent discourse between the two nations.

The long table was a simple yet symbolic statement; it did not make material alterations to the existing space, but it did change the visitor's perception of it.

Objects in the existing building

There is inevitably a direct relationship between the existing building and the new interior. The redesign has to take into consideration the size, shape, proportions, details and materials of the original structure. The resultant interior has, at its beginning, an understanding of the qualities of the already there. The form of the new is based upon the form of the old.

Above:
Circulation
Bridges directly connect the new element with the existing building.

Haus im Haus

Name:
Haus im Haus

Location:
Hamburg, Germany

Date:
2007

Designer:
Behnisch Architekten

Hamburg's Chamber of Commerce occupies an extensive neo-classical building in the heart of the city. It was desperately underutilised and, in 2004, Behnisch Architekten proposed a method of inserting five levels of useful space into the central atrium. A business start-up centre and consultation, exhibition, club and meeting room facilities for members, guests and visitors are all arranged in a sculptural multi-level construction. The architects designed a complex, freestanding, self-contained object to occupy the void at the centre of the building. Each level contains a different activity and the quality of the space is designed to reflect the particular function that takes place within. The open, uppermost level contains a 'roof-top' restaurant.

The language of the new is quite different to that of the old; highly reflective materials such as steel and glass are juxtaposed against stone and render. But the form of this huge single element is based upon the size and the proportions of the existing building. The height and width are constrained by the dimensions of the atrium. The floor levels are dictated by the necessity for horizontal bridges, which link the new to the old. The original clerestory windows, which provide the restaurant with fabulous views across the city, determined the position of the floor.

The new insertion contrasts strongly with the old, but the two are linked. The size, proportion and scale – the form of the original – determined the form of the new element.

Right:
The grand hall
The autonomous,
freestanding element sits
within the spacious hall.

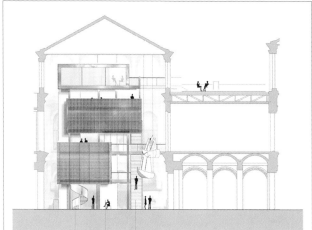

Above:
Plan
The new insertion is built to fit
the scale of the existing building.

Left:
Section
The new element sits within the
side hall of the enormous building.

Methods of organisation > **Form** > Materials

XAP Corporation office

Name:
XAP Corporation office

Location:
Culver City, USA

Date:
2001

Designer:
Pugh + Scarpa Architects

The designer can create a series of distinct forms to act as focal points within a large and relatively simple enclosure. The XAP Corporation is situated in a large industrial building that has an exposed structure and clerestory windows in the saw-tooth roof. Large organic forms were carefully positioned within the austere warehouse, and these house the public or communal activities. The workstations are rigorously simple, and are organised in a straightforward manner. These act as a counterpoint to the sculptural feature elements. The boardroom and conference room are huge, freestanding, organic forms that tower over the rest of the furniture in the double-height space. The steel structure is exposed on the exterior of the forms, while the interiors have a smooth plaster finish. The curved form combined with the direct lighting created intimate spaces with a confidential atmosphere.

The designers have populated the interior with a collection of large related forms, which house the public or communal activities and convey an image of creative activity.

Above:
View through the interior
The collection of installations dominate the large and spacious interior.

Right:
Concept sketch
The rhythm of the room broken into a series of structural layers.

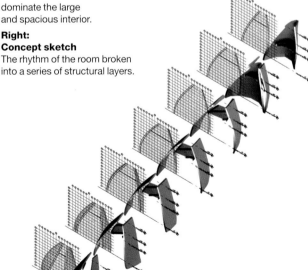

Objects in the existing building

Above:
Conference room
The freestanding organic
form is juxtaposed against
the regular timber structure
of the existing building.

Pugh + Scarpa Architects
Pugh + Scarpa is an American practice
that pursues the need for a sense of
continuity within its work. This is not only
from one project to the next, but also within
the search for meaning and a connection
with the context and the past.

Methods of organisation > **Form** > Materials

Tate Liverpool

Name:
Tate Liverpool
Location:
Liverpool, England
Date:
2008
Designer:
Arca

A building may need to be updated. This may not change the primary function but will perhaps reorder the internal organisation to accommodate the changing needs of the users. One such building, situated in a dramatic setting overlooking the river Mersey, is the Tate Gallery in Liverpool.

The original warehouse, completed in 1848, was a monumental brick and stone building constructed over a colonnade of sturdy Doric columns. In 1988, the architect James Stirling converted the north-west corner of the seven-storey warehouse into a five-storey modern art gallery, the biggest outside London. The rest of the massive U-shaped industrial warehouse block was mostly given over to apartments and retail developments. Stirling's design left the exterior of the building almost untouched but transformed the interior into an arrangement of simple, elegant galleries suitable for the display of modern art.

Twenty years on from the original conversion, Arca were commissioned to reorganise the reception areas. This was to provide improved control of ticketing, education parties and special events. The new spaces were also designed to provide better connection with the refurbished shop and café spaces while externally, the façade was made more visible to visitors. The majority of the works are relatively subtle and subdued, such as facilities for storage and more lighting. However, the main reception desk was designed as a dramatic statement within the large foyer space. It is a long, bright orange, extruded form, which flows theatrically through the space. The architects have created a focal point that epitomises the convergence of business with art. It is a strong and bold element that is very appropriate in a gallery, but is also ergonomically functional.

Above:
The entrance hall
The extruded bright orange reception desk flows through the reception area; it is a dramatic and vivid element within the calm and controlled space.

Objects in the existing building

Arca

Arca are a young and dynamic Manchester-based practice, who regard space, light and materials as the basic blocks of building. They have a holistic approach, in that they are concerned not only with the building, but also with the graphics, lighting, furniture, film, TV and installation art.

Methods of organisiation > **Form** > Materials

The materials that the designer selects can convey the identity of the project. The designer may want to create a strong contrast between old and new; conversely, they may feel it necessary to integrate the two. The choice of material can influence the way in which a space is used; for example, strong and robust finishes will encourage the end-users of the space to use it in a vigorous and forceful manner. The materials can also be used to reflect the function, to contribute to the explanation of the purpose, they may directly illustrate the rationale behind the project.

Siobhan Davies Studios

Name:
Siobhan Davies Studios

Location:
London, England

Date:
2006

Designer:
Sarah Wigglesworth Architects

Dancers are encouraged to respond to the place in which they are dancing. It is important to them to be able to perceive the parameters of the space, so that they are always aware of their own position in connection with the size and nature of the room; hence the expression to centre oneself in the room. They are also acutely aware of the materials from which a space is constructed; the floor must allow them to spring from it and the walls must not feel oppressive.

The Siobhan Davies Studios are situated within a disused boarding school in Southwark, London. The designers felt that it was important to retain the feeling and qualities of the school, and so the majority of the spaces are very much as they were when originally designed in 1898, even down to the ornamental details and the fragments of paintwork. However, the designers have made two very dramatic statements, which drag the building into the twenty-first century and signal the new use. The first is a multi-toned patchwork box attached to the side elevation of the building. This contains a steel-and-glass floating staircase protected by the concrete, glass and timber screen. The other insertion is equally exciting: the top floor of the building was completely cleared to create one huge studio with a sprung floor. A new steel-framed roof was constructed above it, the exterior of which was finished with sky-blue resin and the interior clad with insulated birch-faced plywood panels. The dramatically curving ceiling is both sound-absorbent and warm.

The designers have attached two apparently independent forms to the building, the materials are sympathetic and appropriate to their setting, and yet the dramatic nature of the objects imbues the remodelled building with vigour and life. The dancers can feel happy within and respond to this highly appropriate setting.

Objects in the existing building

Facing page:
Exterior
The blue resin roof floats
above the building, signaling
the change of use.

Above:
Interior of the rooftop
dance hall
The timber finish of the
curving roof panels is both
sound-absorbent and warm.

Below:
Elevation
New and old co-exist happily
side by side.

Above:
The Air Pavilion
This evocative element hovers
in the huge space.

Right:
The Water Pavilion
The design of the pavilion is
intended to represent liquid.

Magna Science Adventure Centre

Name:
Magna Science Adventure Centre

Location:
Rotherham, England

Date:
2001

Designer:
Wilkinson Eyre Architects

The designer can create an object that is wilfully different to the existing space; this has the effect of generating a strong contrast between the new and the old. Each is enhanced by its difference to the other. This is the approach taken by Wilkinson Eyre in their design for the Magna Science Adventure Centre. The museum, which is based in a disused steelworks, houses four different pavilions. Each one contains interactive exhibitions and is dedicated to a particular element: fire, earth, water and air. The pavilions are connected to the host building and are tied together with a metal catwalk. This elevates the visitor far away from the dark and dangerous steelworks floor.

The appearance of each pavilion is intended to evoke the image of its title and reflect the contents of the exhibitions inside. The dirty, detritus-filled interior of the steelworks is in stark contrast to the brilliance of each of these freestanding objects. The Air Pavilion is a 40-metre long, fabric-clad tensile structure that hangs from the roof of the building. Despite its size, the sheer scale of the shed renders it miniature. The shape of the Water Pavilion is intended to suggest a wave; this is accentuated with rings of blue neon. The Fire Pavilion is a matt-black steel box that indicates the hazardous processes taking place within, while the Earth Pavilion, which is fittingly buried in the floor, appears as though carved from solid stone.

The designers have created a dynamic statement about Britain's post-industrial society by generating a dialogue between the decaying remains of the huge steelworks and the dazzling exhibition installations.

Form > **Materials**> Function

Top:
Detail of the decoration
The colours and style of
decoration are appropriate
to their context.

Above:
Column detail
The foliage on the capitals was
kept deliberately unpatterned
to accentuate the complex
organic form of the carving.

Facing page:
The highly decorated apse
The changing intensity
of the decoration combined
with the Gothic style of
architecture encourages
the eye to move upwards.

St Mary of Furness Church

Name:
St Mary of Furness Church

Location:
Barrow-in-Furness, England

Date:
2006

Designer:
Francis Roberts Architects

A particular architectural
element can be revitalised and
invigorated through decoration.
Emphasis can be give to
a specific part of a building
by simple ornamentation and
embellishment. Francis Roberts
Architects are prominent
conservationist architects
with a reputation for a sensitive
approach to the preservation
and remodelling of existing
buildings, as well as the
contextual considerations that
they bring to the construction
of new buildings. They have
taken a particularly tactful and
sympathetic approach to the
conservation and redecoration
of the St Mary of Furness Church
in Cumbria.

The church, which is large,
ornate and Gothic, was designed
by E.W. Pugin. It opened in 1867,
although the tower and steeple
were not completed until 1888.
Francis Roberts Architects found
the interior painted the ubiquitous
off-white that was so popular
in the mid-twentieth century. They
felt that this was an opportunity
to not only restore the church to
its former glory, but also a chance
to embellish, with decoration,
certain elements within the
building. The architects took this
as their cue for the redecoration.
Although the whole building
has been decorated, it is the
polygonal east apse that has been
repainted in a rich and romantic
manner, thus acknowledging
its focus and importance. The
ornamentation is precious
and opulent and it serves
to emphasise the architectural
language of the apse. It is
deliberately more dense and
complex at the base, gradually
becoming more simple and
light as it rises up the interior
walls, thus encouraging the
congregation to lift their eyes
and turn their thoughts towards
the heavens.

Francis Roberts Architects
Francis Roberts Architects use a mixture of traditional
and modern techniques and value collaborations
with artists and craftsmen. This approach is directly
influenced by the work of the Arts and Crafts Movement
and is characterised by a feeling for place translated
into building form, materials and detail.

Form > **Materials** > Function

The functional requirements of the proposed users of a remodelled space need to be fully understood for the designer to be able to create an advantageous integration of the new with the old. The approach that the designer will take will be based on a full understanding of the needs of the end-user. This examination might find that there are a number of overlapping functional needs. For example, a retail unit may need a large space that is supported by a number of much smaller ones; so too will a gallery and possibly office space.

Kodak House

Name:
Kodak House

Location:
Dublin, Ireland

Date:
1998

Designer:
Paul Keogh Architects

The designers have inserted an office into the open, top-lit, upper level of a disused Kodak factory. To be able to function well, Cawley Nea \ TBWA, an advertising agency, required a collection of different types of spaces. They needed a large open office for the sales people, private offices for concentrated work, enclosed meeting rooms and spaces for social interaction. This is an example of the New Office; a system of planning that creates spaces for specific functions rather than for people.

Paul Keogh Architects placed a long, two-storey element through the centre of the double-height space. This effectively divided the room into three. Quiet rooms were created within the formal element and noisy work spaces either side of it. The roof of the controlling element was left open and populated with soft furnishings, thus creating a casual space suitable for informal interaction. This provided the agency with the assortment of different atmospheres that they required.

Above:
View from reception area looking into the office
The two-storey structure, which occupies the centre of the building, controls and orders the accommodation.

Objects in the existing building

Left:
View into foyer area
The casual organisation of
the waiting space is quite different
to the rigid organisation of the
office space.

Below:
Plan
This drawing clearly shows
the different types of space that
have been created within the
advertising agency.

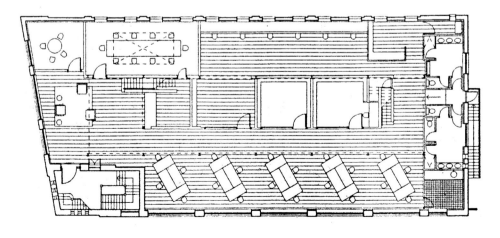

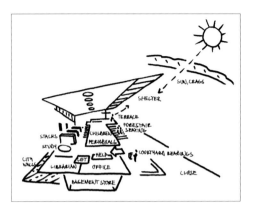

Above:
The site before
construction began
The protective historic
wall encloses and shelters
the library context.

Left:
Staircase
The staircase runs from the
double-height shelving area
up to the reading balcony. The
building gradually rises as it
moves from the rear to the front.

Top left:
Conceptual sketch
This contextual reading shows
how the needs of the users
are combined with the qualities
of the existing site.

'The Library is built to express joy and optimism in the future of poetry within our culture: an engine for cultural renewal rather than a dry container for historical documents.'

Malcolm Fraser Architects

Scottish Poetry Library

Name:
Scottish Poetry Library

Location:
Edinburgh, Scotland

Date:
1999

Designer:
Malcolm Fraser Architects

Projects that entail building reuse are most successful when the designer combines a thorough knowledge of the requirements of the new users with an intimate awareness of the qualities of the site or context.

The Scottish Poetry Library was to be housed in a very limited existing building. Although it was in a very important historical position, almost all of it had disappeared. However, an understanding of the site provided much of the stimulation for the design. It is situated next to the city walls in an area that is a real historical composite, incorporating a sixteenth-century gable end, a fragment of the seventeenth-century city wall and the end of a nineteenth-century warehouse. Malcolm Fraser Architects used this to the advantage of the new users of the building. They regarded the new structure as an insertion that pressed itself closely to the protective city walls and then gradually opened up to the view and the light.

The physically and visually strong city walls support the new steelwork, which spans across the building to the open front. The bookshelves are positioned between the existing eyelets in the original wall. This provides bright streams of natural light in what would otherwise be a dark and oppressive place. The reader selects a book in this intimate and enclosed area before moving across the building into the light to read it.

The designers have used the qualities that were embedded within the site, combined with the needs of the Poetry Library users, to create a building of delicate yet robust sensitivity.

'Only when one stands on the arrow-like structure, walks through it, sees and almost feels how the metal cuts though the stone does one apprehend what the architect Günther Domenig means when he speaks of driving a stake through the flesh of the building.'

Christian Schittich

Documentation Centre, Nazi Party Rally Grounds

Name:
Documentation Centre,
Nazi Party Rally Grounds

Location:
Nuremberg, Germany

Date:
2001

Designer:
Günther Domenig

The manner in which an existing building is remodelled allows the designer to make an ethical statement about the original purpose of the building. The Documentation Centre is situated in Kongresshalle in Nuremberg. Much of the city, which suffered massive damage during the Second World War, was rebuilt but it was difficult to know what to do with the massive Kongresshalle. It wasn't until 1998 that a competition was held to design the documentation centre.

Domenig's approach was to aggressively thrust a steel and glass shaft diagonally through the building, thus shattering the balanced and classical nature of the original building. This uncompromising process undermines the intentions of the earlier structure; it is not a sensitive interpretation but is making a moral statement about the meaning of the former Kongresshalle. The diagonal element, which is 130 metres long and 1.8 metres wide, contains the circulation. Visitors climb on to the element to enter the building and traverse its whole length, before disembarking and wandering back through the galleries to the entrance area. It literally smashes through the walls; no attempt has been made to clean up the internal junctions between old and new, they are left wounded and broken – again an ethical statement of intent. The new function is a declaration that deliberately challenges and destabilises the original use of the building.

Above:
**View through to
the reception area**
The steel and glass elements of circulation converge at this point.

Objects in the existing building

Left:
Entrance
The junction between the existing building and the new additions are left raw and exposed: a contemporary commentary on the ideology of the previous function.

Responsive objects can be described as those
that are deliberately designed to occupy a specific
position. For example, an exhibition stand could
be constructed to fill a particular place in a museum
and it could only go in that position as it would not
fit or be appropriate anywhere else. Other examples
include fitted furniture, such as that found in the
kitchen or the bathroom, insertions that may contain
complete rooms or even art installations. These
are described as responsive because the form
and nature of the element or object respond directly
to the qualities of the space that it is to occupy.
These are not pieces of furniture that are selected
for a specific place, but one-off designs that are
intended to inhabit an exact location.

Name:
Völklingen Ironworks
(see pp 114+115)

Location:
Völklingen, Germany

Date:
1994

Designer:
Johann Peter Luth

Objects in the existing building > **Responsive objects: built to fit** > Autonomous objects: stand alone

Human scale

Small-sized objects are generally designed to accommodate intimate human needs. They respond to the scale of a person; for example, a seat must be comfortable, a display or exhibition stand needs to be at the required height and a shop counter should be accessible. These smaller-scale objects may be part of a much larger installation or design. They are sometimes just one element within a larger collection, and therefore respond not just to their situation, but also to the other elements within the series.

Room scale

Medium-sized objects are of a larger scale and can be designed as a complete unit. This may be as an individual display within a huge exhibition, such as the Ideal Home Exhibition. Or the room-sized element could be the room itself; for example, a dining room could be designed as a single installation. Responsive objects and elements of this scale are sensitive to the enclosing building but are also designed with the scale and needs of the individual user in mind.

Building scale

Large-sized objects are often single elements that dominate a space. These may be a number of functions collected together in a substantially sized unit, which is carefully positioned within an existing or proposed building. An even larger-scale approach is the responsive addition to an existing building that is bigger than the original structure. A single, huge element can completely envelope the old construction, leaving it as the enigmatic, freestanding element.

Responsive objects: built to fit

Above:
l.a. Eyeworks, Los Angeles, USA
(see pp 108+109).

A well-designed piece of furniture can be a sculptural element within a collection of forms and materials. It can act in an architectural manner, controlling space and directing movement. It can express human scale while also relating to the architectural scale of a building and it can be created in a totally modern language while still being completely appropriate to its surroundings.

Above:
Lifeline
A written chronology of the life of Churchill is inscribed on to a long, back-illuminated table.

Churchill Museum

Name:
Churchill Museum

Location:
London, England

Date:
2005

Designer:
Casson Mann

Exhibition design can reinforce a theme; the designer may create an atmosphere within the gallery that evokes the character of the subject being displayed. This is the approach taken by Casson Mann to the design of Churchill Museum, which is situated within the Cabinet War Rooms at the Imperial War Museum in London. The exhibition provides a rich mix that invites interactive investigation into the actions, thoughts, interests and relationships of the man voted the Greatest Briton by the British public. The space is shadowy and slightly oppressive. The ceiling is low, the structure and the services exposed, the floor is dark parquet; the room feels strong, intense and protected. This is all highly suggestive of a World War Two operations room.

This intense room has been populated with a series of related elements, which respond both to the slightly oppressive nature of the rooms and the subject itself. Long, low, bottom-lit tables are arranged with military precision to respond to the structural grid of the space, hinting at the style that would have been used in strategy and operations meetings. The low levels of ambient lighting and the deep colours of the floor, walls and ceiling encourage the visitor to focus upon these 18-metre long interactive elements. A huge virtual archive, known as the 'Lifeline', is housed within them. Objects to read, to listen to, to watch, to touch and to smell are arranged in layers, thus enabling the visitor to engage with and control the amount of information that they want to receive.

Casson Mann has developed an incredibly evocative method of presenting the thousands of documents associated with Churchill. Both the display cabinets and the gallery reinforce the intense, passionate and powerful qualities of the great man.

Responsive objects: built to fit

MEN OF OLDHAM
VOTE FOR
CHURCHILL
AND
CRISP
WHO ARE
TOP OF THE CARD
AND WILL BE
TOP OF THE POLL

Above:
The bunker
The quality of the interior space
is reminiscent of a Second
World War operations room.

Right:
The exhibition
The room is organised with
military precision.

Above:
The foyer
The cornice of the Royal Academy main galleries now forms part of a long, low sculpture plinth.

Sackler Galleries, Royal Academy of Arts

Name:
Sackler Galleries,
Royal Academy of Arts

Location:
London, England

Date:
1991

Designer:
Foster + Partners

A small interpretive detail can contain the design ethos of the complete space. The manner in which one element is treated can reflect the approach taken by the designer to the entire interior.

Foster + Partners were commissioned to create galleries from an attic space in the Royal Academy. The biggest problem was not the design of the galleries themselves, but that of providing access to the new space. Foster + Partners requisitioned the gap or lightwell between the original building, Burlington House, and the Garden House extension. This gap of just over four metres provided the perfect space for the stairs and the lift – the vertical circulation between the ground floor and the rooftop Sackler Galleries.

A finely crafted, square section steel and glass balcony was placed right at the top of the lightwell; indeed, the cornice of the Royal Academy main galleries was transformed into a long, low sculpture plinth. A small resting corner was formed within the quiet area behind the glass and steel staircase. This calm and thoughtful space was created by continuing the suspended floor of the foyer, but the reposeful character was reinforced by a change in materials. The new element is a substantial solid stone bench, constructed from blocks of limestone and set into the cornice of the original building. This element acts to direct the eye around the corner of the space and thus create a strong end or edge to the space, as well as offer an opportunity for the visitor to rest. The strong scale of the element is appropriate to its surroundings and the materials reflect the exquisite qualities of the whole space. This is fitted furniture at its most robust.

Responsive objects: built to fit

'The architectural dignity which Foster gives the more mundane part of his brief – circulation – connects the more exalted – the exhibits – with external realities that give them more power and more sense.'

Rowan Moore

Above:
The balustrade
A square section steel and glass balcony was placed right at the top of the lightwell.

Left:
The seat
A small resting corner, formed from solid limestone, creates a quiet area behind the glass and steel staircase.

Above:
TV monitors
The screens broadcast the images upside down; this disconnects the viewer from those being viewed.

'Para-Site' exhibition

Name:
'Para-Site' exhibition

Location:
New York, USA

Date:
1989

Designer:
Diller Scofidio + Renfro

Even relatively small objects can be designed to connect disparate parts of an interior together. Although they are not large and therefore cannot physically make the link, they can generate connections between areas of the building that are separated by distance or structure. This can provoke an affinity between places and spaces. This was the approach taken by Diller Scofidio + Renfro when creating their installation, 'Para-Site', for the Museum of Modern Art in New York. The designers developed a televisual link between an internal gallery space and the entrance areas of the museum, thus creating a direct relationship between the visitors within the gallery space and those who were just entering the building.

This temporary exhibition used the visitor as the subject matter; they were observed and recorded from three locations within the museum's circulation system. The recorded images were relayed to a series of monitors installed within the gallery. A spider-like timber and steel structure attached to the ceiling of the gallery space held the TV screens in place. The installation looked like an animal of some description that had invaded the gallery and clamped itself into position. Also attached to the ceiling was an ordinary wooden dining room chair, placed upside down. This was because it was a representation of the viewer, a symbolic portrayal of the museum visitor.

This instinctive, almost primordial, human-scale collection of objects is a small expressive representation of the gallery and its visitors.

'Para-Site is a site specific installation [that] takes up the theme of a filtered vision in the museum. As parasiting is by nature site specific, a closer reading of the organism is unavoidable.'

Elizabeth Diller
Richard Scofidio

Below:
The exhibition
The insect-like structures that receive the images from disparate parts of the museum are suspended from the walls and ceiling of the gallery.

Elements and objects of a fairly large scale generally act in one of two ways. The first is as a freestanding or independent object; this may take the form of a complete room or function. The second is an element that serves to tie a series of distinct areas or actions together. This could be a complete floor, a wall or an element, which changes as it flows through a space.

Grand Central bar

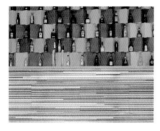

Above:
The bar counter
The aesthetic of the bar was directly influenced by car tail lights racing through the night-time streets outside.

Name:
Grand Central bar

Location:
London, England

Date:
2001

Designer:
Block Architecture

A single element can tie a number of different spaces and activities together. Grand Central is situated in a high, L-shaped space on a busy corner site in Shoreditch, London. The oddly shaped interior forms a collection of dissimilar spaces rather than one united space. This condition was exploited by the designers to generate a series of little areas, each with varying degrees of intimacy. The designers tied all the separate spaces together with a single flowing element. A wall of light seems to drift around the wine bar. It begins and ends at the door, running around the space, separating and defining the distinct areas.

The designers describe this as a process that uses light, movement and electricity as physical building elements, to create an environment based on city flux. They were influenced by long exposure photography of traffic flow. The light-stream walls are constructed from strips of live edge and coloured Perspex that have been laminated together and back-lit. This imitates the effect of the extruded light paths produced by the head and tail lights of passing cars.

Although the wall that runs through the space is broken, it appears to be a complete element that unites the disparate spaces within the room.

Above:
The bar
The wall of light races around
the space.

Live edge perspex
Live edge perspex is a sheet polymer that contains
fluorescent dyes. Light is transmitted through
the sheet, and is much more intense at the edges.
If lit from one side, the other edge appears to glow.

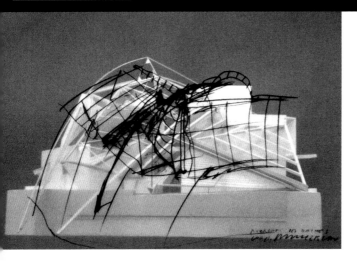

Left:
Sketch
The dramatic concept of the rooftop remodelling.

Schuppich, Sporn & Winischhofer offices

Name:
Schuppich, Sporn and Winischhofer offices

Location:
Vienna, Austria

Date:
1988

Designer:
Coop Himmelblau

A single, surprising element can generate a progressive atmosphere of creativity and dynamism. This was the impression that a chamber of lawyers were keen to communicate when they appointed Coop Himmelblau to redevelop the top floor meeting room in their building.

The designers placed a vigorous irregular covering over the rooftop space. The steel and glass form is reminiscent of a huge bird that is just about to alight upon the building. The element radically reinterprets the question of what a roof is for and what its function really is.

The rooftop object is hardly visible from the ground; all that can be seen from that level is a small, tail-like section that protrudes over the edge of the cornice. It is from the interior, upon entering the room, that the visitor receives the full impact of this radical and extraordinary element. The spine of the new element seems to spring asymmetrically from close to the corner of the building, and rise over the space to lean upon new columns at the edge. The glazed structure sits slightly out of line with the original ridge and barely touches the building. The new roof gives impressive views across the Vienna skyline, which it too, in turn has drastically altered. It gives the impression that anything is possible.

Above:
Interior view
The traditional conference
table is a more sober reminder
of the function of the space.

Coop Himmelblau
Coop Himmelblau, a practice formed
in 1968, have always questioned the
strategies that govern human action
and interaction. Much of this is derived
from the teachings of Derrida and the
deconstructivist movement. Their refusal
to accept predetermined solutions has
given them an international reputation
as architects who continually surprise.

Human scale > **Room scale** > Building scale

Above:
The reception
The counter is integral to the linear folding element.

Facing page:
Retail space
The organic element rolls through the space before folding down to become a display counter.

'Denari has been a leader in his generation's use of advanced technology to propose architecture that shifts, bends, folds and unfolds, always challenging conventional geometry with pure beauty and a quality he refers to as "cultural sustainability".'

Neil M. Denari

l.a. Eyeworks

Name:
l.a. Eyeworks

Location:
Los Angeles, USA

Date:
2002

Designer:
Neil M. Denari Architects (NMDA)

Neil M. Denari Architects have a reputation for creating innovative and exciting design solutions. Whatever the particular functional requirements of a project, they regard each commission as an experiment that attempts to redirect expectations toward new and even better forms of functional and aesthetic performance.

The vision for the l.a. Eyeworks store in Los Angeles was based upon a balance between the conventional demands of a commercial retail practice and the dynamic identity of the fashion company. This design satisfies all the normal retail requirements, such as the need for a transparent window display, sales and display counters and signage. However this is achieved with one gracefully twisting sinuous element. A gaseous blue surface winds its way though the length of the shop, changing its form, alignment and purpose as it goes. It performs many functions: perforated ceiling plane; window display; bench; shelving unit and sales counter.

The design of this multifunctional element shapes space and movement though a continuous suspended surface. It is both efficient and inventive. It merges the functional demands of an eyewear store with the ambitions of high fashion.

Freestanding objects and elements can be of such a large size that they are as big or even bigger that the original building. This creates a strange balance between the old and the new; each has the strength of size. Massive additions to existing buildings can sometimes act as extensions, although they would normally be regarded as buildings in their own right, unless they are integrated with the original building.

Landau Public Library

Name:
Landau Public Library

Location:
Landau, Germany

Date:
1998

Designer:
Lamott Architeken BDA

The old slaughterhouse in Landau was once regarded as a landmark, celebrated for its grandeur. However, the fact that it was positioned close to the town centre and needed to be modernised meant that the building was closed and remodelled as the public library at the end of the twentieth century.

The strategy that the designers took was to remove any later additions and so return the buildings to their original form. They completely wrapped these remaining structures in an enclosing wall of steel and glass. This new construction contrasts strongly with the old sandstone and brick. The low, modern, enclosing shed is a different size, shape and construction to the taller, late-nineteenth-century buildings. This allows both structures to appear almost independent of each other, yet they act in a complementary manner; each seems to balance and accentuate the other.

The slaughterhouse buildings are treated as the objects in space; they control the organisation of the internal accommodation, while the new enclosing glass wall promotes transparency, admits light and provides the services. The original buildings have become the freestanding elements, enigmatically contained within a busy and modern shell.

Above:
The children's library
The louvres in front of the windows shelter the space from excessive solar gain.

Responsive objects: built to fit

Above:
The main library
The room is rigorously
organised around the structure
of the existing building.

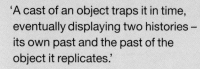

'A cast of an object traps it in time, eventually displaying two histories – its own past and the past of the object it replicates.'

Richard Shone

Above:
Simulacrum
The natural order of the house was reversed.

Facing page:
The sculpture
Once the existing walls were peeled away, all that was left was a solidification of the life of the interior.

House

Name:
House

Location:
London, England

Date:
1993 (temporary work)

Designer:
Rachel Whiteread

The approach that an artist takes towards the remodelling of an existing building can often prove influential. Rachel Whiteread, winner of the Turner Prize in 1993, is one such artist. The manner in which she works and the bold and striking sculptures that she constructs have given her an international reputation.

Whiteread casts space; she makes solid representations of nothing. But in doing this, she exposes and makes vulnerable hidden and secret areas. *House* was a casting of the interior of a single terraced property in London. The whole row was due to be demolished and Whiteread chose a house from the middle of the row. The sculpture is not actually completely solid, the interior of the building was sprayed with concrete and when this was set, the exterior walls were removed, leaving just the freestanding three-dimensional form.

House was more than just a copy of what was there, it was a simulacrum: a representation or an image. The natural order of the house was reversed; the negative became positive and the positive, negative. The space, the areas of occupation, the transparent rooms that were previously filled with air, furniture and people became solidified. They were opaque and impenetrable. They were exposed; every mark, notch and dent was described. The casting was inside out, almost as if the visitor viewed the details, the ornamentation and the relief from behind, from the wrong side.

When the art piece was constructed, it proved to be extremely controversial. It was considered by many influential people to be impolite and improper. It was regarded as a piece that had no respect for society and was contemptuous of the notion of the home. As a result of public and journalistic pressure, *House* was demolished in 1994.

'I know of no comparable project in the whole world where one can go so far into its mediation and staging as well as the maintenance and transformation of industrial cultural grounds as the World Cultural Heritage Site Voelklinger.'

Dr Wolfgang Ebert

Völkingen Ironworks

Name:
Völklingen Ironworks

Location:
Völklingen, Germany

Date:
1994

Designer:
Johann Peter Luth

The disused *Völklinger Hütte* (Völkingen Ironworks) dominates the town after which it is named. It covers some six acres, rises to over 45 metres high and is visible from everywhere in the city. It had its beginnings in 1873 at the height of the Industrial Revolution and gradually expanded until, in 1965, over 17,000 people worked there. Two decades later, deeply affected by the worldwide steel crisis and the gradual de-industrialisation of all western societies, Völkingen Ironworks closed. In 1994, UNESCO declared it a World Heritage site; it is the only surviving ironworks in the world from the heyday of iron and steel production and is a unique testimony to an industrial epoch of the past.

A visit to the Völklingen Ironworks is a post-industrial adventure; it is a journey down deep into the dark corridors of the burden shed and up to the lofty heights of the blast furnace viewing platform. The visitor is led on a 5,000-metre journey around the works, through the world's largest sintering plant, past the blast furnaces, over the ore shed, into the blower hall, in front of the coking plant, culminating in the ferrodron. The route is prescribed; a carefully placed walkway directs and controls movement. The design of these bridges and paths reflects the brutal and industrial landscape that they inhabit. They can be regarded as a single element that ties all the different areas of the steelworks together.

The visitors are almost like the product; they enter at one end, experience a number of different processes and emerge at the other end. Tourism flourishes in this post-industrial playground.

Top:
Silhouette
The abandoned steelworks make a dramatic statement on the skyline.

Above:
New balcony
The language of the new elements reflects the raw industrial landscape.

Facing page:
The rusty remains
The sculptural quality of the plant is emphasised by the silence.

Matthew Hilton Design Studio
with Remploy Limited
Flexible table

Autonomous objects can be described as those
that are designed without consideration for their
specific end location. They are elements that can
be placed in and would be suitable for a number
of different positions. Furniture is the most obvious
example of this approach; a specific chair can be
situated in many different places without losing its
identity. Indeed, the designer may select a particular
piece of furniture to imbue identity upon a given
interior. Of course, the autonomous object is
capable of responding to its given position although
it wasn't specifically designed to occupy it.

Name:
'Furniture for the Future'
exhibition (see pp 126+127)

Location:
London, England

Date:
2003

Designer:
Softroom with Marc Jacobs

Human scale

These are objects that are scaled to accommodate the needs of a person. Certain ergonomic considerations will have been taken into account. The seat of a chair is at a certain height from the ground, as are desktops. Exhibition stands are elevated to a position where the exhibits can be easily viewed and storage units are designed to make the contents easily accessible.

Room scale

These medium-sized elements must respond to the needs of the human users of a space, but also have sufficient magnitude to not be overwhelmed by the room or surroundings. The room-sized object may be an exhibition stand, for example, intended to project a particular brand or product. This would normally be one amongst hundreds at a trade fair or exposition, so would therefore need to have sufficient magnitude to be noticed and stand out in the midst of the other competing units.

Building scale

Large-sized objects are normally site specific; they are designed to occupy or even fill a precise position. However, there are a number of exceptions to this, the pavilion being a good example. It is a small temporary building that is intended to convey a particular message. It will usually have a short lifespan, it may even be demountable, that is it can be taken apart and reassembled in a different location.

Facing page:
Hairywood summer house,
London, England
(see pp 132+133).

Autonomous objects: stand alone

HAIRYWOOD

A functional element of human scale can possess the ability to be both useful and sculptural. Single pieces of furniture have always been imbued with artistic qualities; they can easily become the focal point within a room or space. For example, Mies van der Rohe's Barcelona Pavilion Chair is regarded as a design classic and, as such, will lend a particular gravitas to a space.

Right:
Chair-stool-bench
The freestanding elements reflect the language of the farmhouse kitchen.

Stuhlhockerbank

Name:
Stuhlhockerbank
(Chair Stool Bench)

Location:
N/A

Date:
2007

Designer:
Yvonne Fehling and Jenny Peiz

A particular piece of furniture can reflect the environment that it inhabits by adopting the same particular attitude that emanates from the space. It can reflect and reinforce the particular character of the building or interior; the furniture can look like it belongs to or with a specific establishment. However, if the furniture is not fixed, it has the possibility of being positioned almost anywhere within that building.

The Stuhlhockerbank collection is a series of extraordinary pieces of furniture that were designed specifically to inhabit the Arp Museum near Bonn, in Germany. Each piece is both contemporary and traditional, in that each uses the language of a conventional farmhouse kitchen chair but subverts it in a postmodern way. The chairs, which are scattered throughout the museum, are arranged in an apparently haphazard manner. But when viewed more closely, the seemingly random relationship between the different chairs is actually fixed and deliberate. Each installation is a collection of timber chair-backs and legs, which are tied together at seat level. Each piece is different, ranging from just two chairs joined with traditionally shaped seats, to large units containing eight or nine chair-backs tied together with a flat bench.

The pieces are both formal and informal; they reference the history and tradition of useful furniture while also suggesting the more pluralistic contemporary society of the twenty-first century.

Top:
Detail
The informality of the objects belies their carefully crafted design.

Above:
Hybrid
The individual parts of the furniture are positioned to provoke conversation.

Introduction > **Human scale** > Room scale

Autonomous objects: stand alone

...riety of public
...ngs including lecture halls and hospitals.

1935 Prouvé turns to architecture for the first time
and working with the architects Marcel Lods and Eugène
Beaudouin designs the metal-framed Aéro-Club, Roland
Garros, near Versailles.

1935-39 Again in collaboration with Beaudouin, Lods and
the engineer Vladimir Bodiansky constructs the Maison
du Peuple and market hall in Clichy.

1939 The French army commissions Prouvé to produce
prefabricated barrack units.

1940-45 Prouvé j...
the liberation   ...istance and after
Produces eme...   Mayor of Nancy.

'Jean Prouvé always regarded himself as more of an engineer and constructor instead of a modern designer. He never designed for the sake of form alone, concentrating instead on the essence of materials, connections and production.'

Le Musée Jean Prouvé

Standard Chair

Name:
Standard Chair

Location:
N/A

Date:
1934

Designer:
Jean Prouvé

A particular piece of furniture can represent a particular age. The Standard Chair by Jean Prouvé is representative of the optimistic period of the mid-1930s. Jean Prouvé was a designer renowned for his ability to combine the tactile qualities of the hand-crafted object with the industrial nature of the manufactured element. He is prized as one of the most innovative architectural and furniture designers of the twentieth century. His intimate knowledge of production allowed him to develop progressive lightweight constructions, which ranged from movable or dismountable furniture to multifunctional façade systems that were intended to clad industrial buildings.

Prouvé developed the Standard Collection of dining room furniture. This was based upon the use of sheet metal and bent plywood. The metal was bent, compressed and then welded. Ergonomic considerations led Prouvé to design the chairs with strong, thick back legs; this is where the chair takes most weight and strain. The front legs, which were constructed from tubular steel, were more elegant and slender to reflect the uneven forces in the manner in which a chair is used. The chair is still in production today.

It was typical of Prouvé to develop the furniture from the scientific principles of weight distribution, combined with knowledge of industrial processes of mass production. This led to the fabrication of objects that are very agreeable. To return again to the Vitruvian principle of 'Commodity, Firmness and Delight', these small, industrially-made, strong and useful objects can still, at the beginning of the twenty-first century, provoke great satisfaction within the user.

Above:
The chair exhibited
When viewed from the side, the difference in the strength of the front and back legs is made obvious.

Facing page:
The Standard Chair
The chair was designed using the ergonomic principles of comfort combined with weight distribution.

Introduction > **Human scale** > Room scale

'We wanted to reset the iconic language of the workplace design by saying we are designing a table, not a table for work.'

Ronan Bouroullec and Erwan Bouroullec

Joyn office system

Name:
Joyn office system

Location:
N/A

Date:
2002

Designer:
Bouroullec Brothers for Vitra

Office furniture is typically fairly anonymous; its design is usually dictated by ergonomic considerations, combined with the need to blend in and not offend. Vitra is one of the few furniture manufacturers that actually encourage designers to experiment with the basic concept of what furniture is. The company promotes excellence in design but manages to combine it with well-designed, user-friendly, comfortable and safe creations. Vitra regards itself as a laboratory that provides designers with the freedom to create experimental furniture objects and interior installations.

The Bouroullec Brothers were approached by Vitra to develop a range of office furniture for the twenty-first century; furniture that was in direct opposition to what was currently being produced. The designers found that most office interiors were dealing with the enormous impact of technology in the workplace by replicating its image with shiny metallic surfaces. The designers declared that their aim was to de-specify furniture, to create multi-task products. They felt that the manner in which furniture was designed was too prescriptive, it only allowed people to work in one particular way; it didn't encourage creativity, lateral thinking or serendipity. They developed a product that they describe as a 'common table', one that allows people to communicate, to complete communal work. They started with the old concept of the big family table, at which everyone sat and everything happened.

The advent of the wireless office, combined with the reduction in the size of technological equipment, has enabled the designers to reclaim the surface of the table; no longer is it cluttered with cables, plugs and massive machines. Instead, it can now be arranged with objects that matter: books, pictures and artefacts that interest and stimulate thought, interaction and productivity.

Autonomous objects: stand alone

Top left:
Detail
Wireless technology has enabled
all sorts of activities to happen
in the same environment.

Above:
The Joyn office system
The table is one piece in a whole
family of different products,
all of which are designed
to complement each other.

Top right:
The big communal table
Vertical dividers can provide
privacy and concentration.

An autonomous unit of a medium size is often a temporary freestanding object that has to function independently of the other elements in the immediate vicinity. It is usually something that is designed to be constructed off-site and merely assembled at the required location. In common with many autonomous objects, the functional requirements of the piece are frequently the most important consideration within the design. How it is to be used and the message that it is imparting is often the over-riding design generator. However, medium-sized objects do need to respond to the space that they inhabit; they should have sufficient magnitude so they are not overwhelmed, while still responding to the needs of the individual user.

Above:
The transportable stand
The demountable exhibition can be reconfigured within any suitably scaled space.

'Furniture for the Future' exhibition

Name:
'Furniture for the Future' exhibition

Location:
London, England

Date:
2003

Designer:
Softroom with Martin Jacobs

Softroom is an innovative and distinct architectural practice whose work encompasses a broad range of sectors and media, including retail, offices, restaurants, exhibitions and even virtual environments. Despite this diversity, all its work is saturated with a twenty-first century sense of adventure and innovation combined with an attention to detail and professionalism.

'Furniture for the Future' was a touring Design Council exhibition that explored the idea of the classroom of the future. The interactive exhibition stand, which was intended to be shown at a number of different locations, was easily demountable. It was designed to be able to be packed away in a lorry before being transported to the next exhibition. The stand itself had to be noticeable in an exhibition hall full of other similar-sized display stands. Softroom deliberately designed a fairly austere setting, which initially looked as though it had very little happening on it. However, when the visitor was invited to sit on a specially designed connected chair beneath the orthogonal exhibition stands, they entered a virtual, interactive environment.

Autonomous objects: stand alone

Above:
The display
The austere display stand
is prominent within the
exhibition hall.

Right:
The library
The folded steel screen
protects this quiet space.

KMS Design Agency office

Name:
KMS Design Agency office

Location:
Munich, Germany

Date:
2000

Designer:
Lynx Architecture

Objects of a substantial size
can control space and movement
within a much larger environment.
Lynx Architecture took this
approach to the design of the
design agency, KMS Team,
in Munich. The large, disused
factory space was stripped
back to the bare walls, which
were then painted white, and
the concrete floor was polished.
Natural light, pouring in from
the enormous full-height windows
that fill the front façade of the
building, dominates the space.
The majority of the work areas
are arranged in a traditional
orthogonal manner; many
rows of desks are separated
by screens.

The library and canteen, however,
have been designed as dramatic
set pieces. The café was raised by
about 200mm, on an apparently
floating concrete slab populated
by a series of elegant timber
benches and long, slender tables.
Opposite the café is the office
library. This is enclosed in a large
channel of rusted steel that is also
raised up from the factory floor.
The steel is used to form the floor
of the library and is then folded up
on one side to enclose the quiet
reading area. On one side are
the book stacks and on the other,
the long, maple reading table.

The two units provide the office
with a focus and control the
circulation through the space.
The offices were deliberately
given a fairly anonymous quality
before identity and character
was imposed through the two
balancing elements.

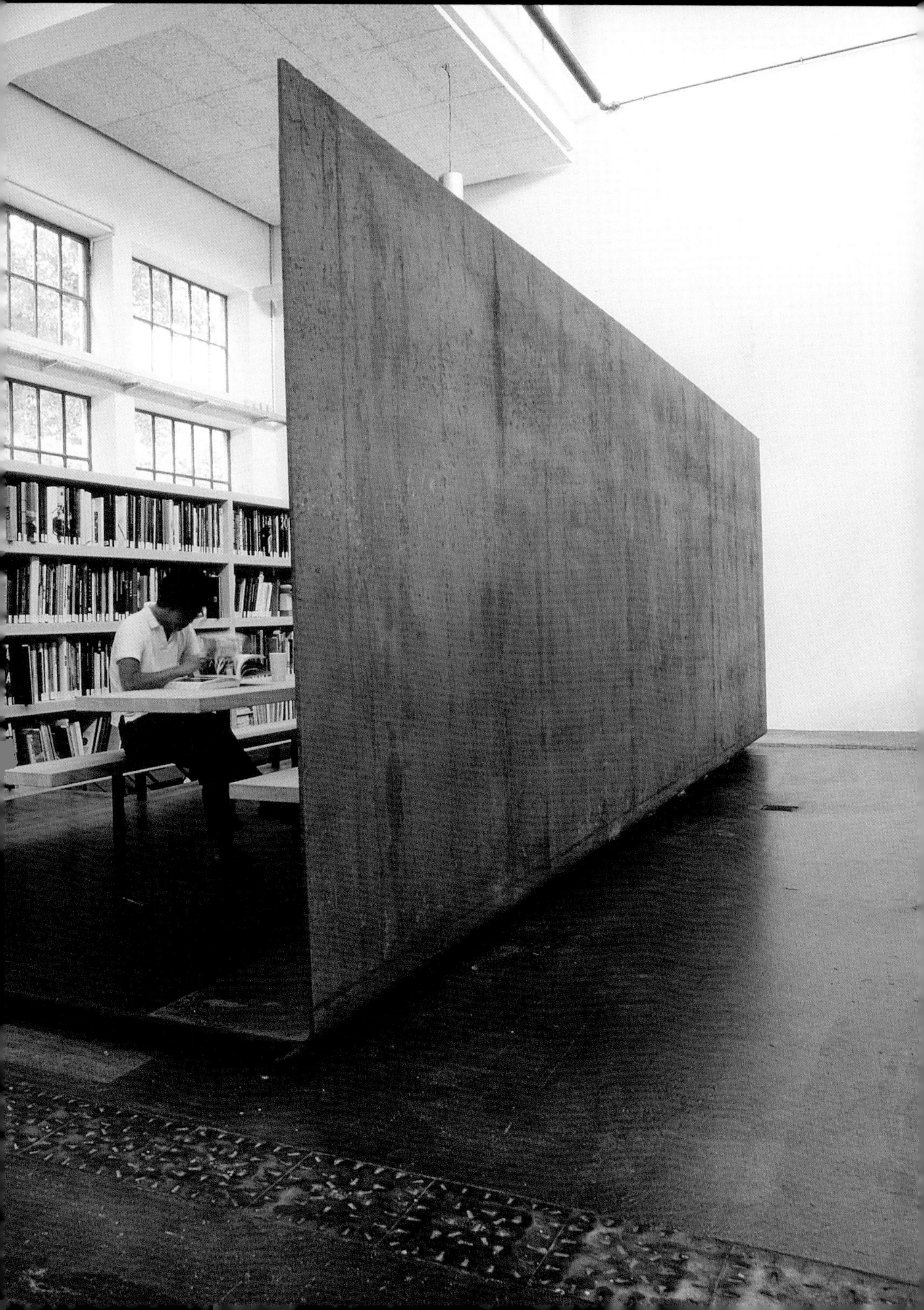

Autonomous objects: stand alone

Top:
The memorial
As the light changes throughout the day, the words and messages are reflected into the darkened chamber.

Above:
The blue chamber
The solemnity of the room is alleviated by the light pouring in from the glass cylinder.

Right:
The cylinder
Words and messages of
sympathy and condolence
are etched on to the glass
block cylinder.

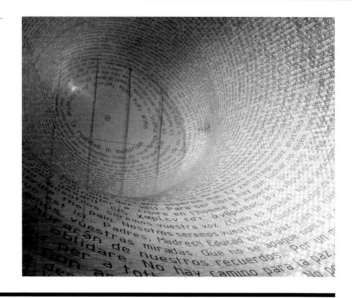

Atocha Memorial

Name:
Atocha Memorial

Location:
Madrid, Spain

Date:
2007

Designer:
Studio fam

An autonomous object can possess its own integrity and independence, while still relating to its environment. It may not always have a direct physical connection with a place, but by virtue of being situated within a space, the object can develop a relationship with it.

In Madrid, Studio fam have designed a monumental and fitting memorial for the 191 victims of the 2004 train bombings. The 11-metre-tall cylinder rises above Atocha station, the destination of the four trains that were targeted, and is conceived as a glowing beacon of remembrance and hope.

The monument is formed out of two 'rooms'; the underground chamber and the tall cylinder. The chamber is entered via Atocha station through a set of glass and steel doors that are inscribed with the names of the victims.

The ceiling, floor and walls of the dark subterranean chamber are painted in blue, and the room is empty, apart from a steel bench. The cylinder rises from the chamber and allows light to pour into the space. The glass walls are etched with the hundreds of messages of condolence and as the sunlight passes through the tower, the words and sympathies sparkle and reflect into the darkened space below. During the day, the sunlight is bright and strong and makes the cylinder glow, while in the evening, as the sun sets, the tower has an ethereal glow and the words are bathed in a melancholy twilight.

This is a remarkable and appropriate memorial that fills the visitor with hope as the darkened chamber is filled with light and the messages of love and sympathy are radiated within it.

A large-scale autonomous element is usually a freestanding object, which is often situated next to a particular building. The object often acts as a signpost or entry porch to signal a particular event or happening. A pavilion is a particularly good example of this type of project; it has a very limited lifespan, just the extent of the event. To aid the speed of construction, it is often assembled from pre-made pieces. The fact that only partial weatherproofing is needed also contributes to the ephemeral quality of the piece.

Hairywood summer house

Name:
Hairywood summer house

Location:
London, England

Date:
2005 (temporary work)

Designer:
6a Architects and Eley Kishimoto

A dramatic exterior installation can indicate that something unusual is happening. A temporary structure has a limited lifespan, maybe just as long as the event itself, and can contribute to the creation of the ambience and atmosphere of the event.

In collaboration with Eley Kishimoto, 6a Architects designed a temporary public space and a landmark. The Architecture Foundation commissioned the structure and it was intended to communicate the arrival of their new gallery on Old Street. The summer house was inspired by a bay window that features in Jaque Tati's film, *Les Vacances de Monsieur Hulot* (1953); Martine, the heroine of the film, gazes out from this window each summer morning before descending noisily through the house, reappearing again at the front door. The small, two-part structure was positioned in the forecourt of the Old Street building. The rear section contained a type of waiting room with long benches positioned against each wall. The front, which was a tower, created a threshold into the new gallery space and offered a place to escape and watch the world go by.

The lower area contained little more than a staircase, which wound up to the small space at the top. This intimate and slightly secret area was intended to resemble a fragment of private space open to the street. The structure was constructed from a timber frame clad with perforated plywood; the interior was lined with printed timber and upholstery. The flowing floral patterns cut into the plywood were especially dramatic at night, when the tower was lit from within, making it glow like a lantern.

This delightful little summer house defined the space while offering a temporary signal to the new gallery.

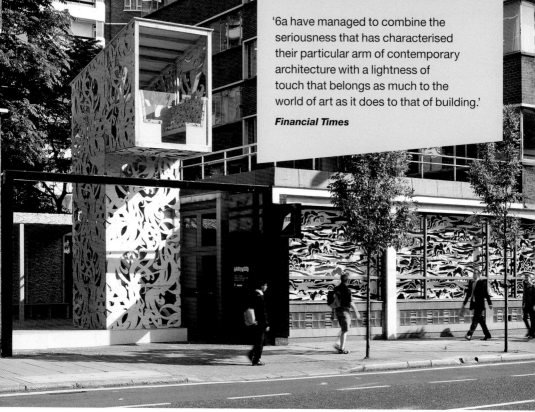

'6a have managed to combine the seriousness that has characterised their particular arm of contemporary architecture with a lightness of touch that belongs as much to the world of art as it does to that of building.'

Financial Times

Above:
Temporary installation
The summer house was positioned to advertise the new gallery. Note the lounge area at the top.

Facing page:
Detail
The flowing floral patterns were cut into the plywood facing.

Right:
Section
The structure contained just two spaces: the stairs and the high sitting room.

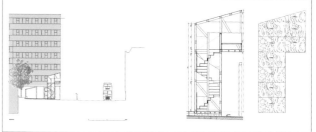

Above:
The pavilion
The uncertain, organic and swirling structure forms an organic landmark within an orthogonal environment.

Left:
Module system
The pavilion was constructed from a module system of almost identical elements: small plywood pieces that were bolted together to form a much greater whole.

'The aim is to experiment with – and exploit to the full – the imaginative spatial and material effects that can be extracted from new-found techniques.'

Charles Walker and Martin Self

Swoosh Pavilion

Name:
Swoosh Pavilion

Location:
London, England

Date:
2008 (temporary work)

Designer:
Unit 2 students,
AA School of Architecture

A purposefully placed object is loaded with meaning; whether it is a small piece of furniture or a large sculpture, it establishes a physical and cultural relationship with its environment. It can influence the way in which the space is viewed; it can deflect the eye towards something else; it can form a focal point or even a landmark.

The Swoosh Pavilion, designed by students at the AA School, is such a purposely placed object. It was positioned on the corner of Bedford Square in London and became a pivotal point in the journey through the open space. The temporary pavilion was sculptural, the flowing shape marked the corner, it provided a point of interest and became a landmark, but was also an object that was part of a journey. The uncertain, organic and swirling shape of the pavilion added a quality of ambivalence to the object. It was non-directional, in that it did not face in any specific direction; it did not address any particular aspect of the square or indeed reference the school itself, although it was only a short distance from it. It was completely self-reverential, the two sloping sides swirling around the central void.

The pavilion was constructed from a module system of small elements, all of which were bolted together to form a much greater whole. The smallest plywood pieces were all virtually identical and served to tie the sculpture together, while the flowing shape was formed by the much larger arched curving vertical elements. The pavilion was used for sitting on, for meeting friends; it marked the corner of the space and formed an organic landmark in amongst the orthogonal environment.

'People think our work is monumental because it's art, but human beings do much bigger things: they build giant airports, highways for thousands of miles, much, much bigger than what we create. It appears to be monumental only because it's art.'

Christo and Jeanne-Claude

The Gates

Name:
The Gates

Location:
New York, USA

Date:
2005 (temporary work)

Designer:
Christo and Jeanne-Claude

A series or collection of matching elements can together create a single dramatic statement. The same object repeated again and again can generate a narrative or journey; it can create a visual link between one area and another, while also guiding a physical journey.

Christo and Jeanne-Claude are artists who make massive installations; they use the existing context to create dramatic statements. They will heighten and make more obvious particular characteristics of the already-there, while removing or reducing other distinctive elements. They are well known for wrapping complete buildings, thus removing the individual details, but accentuating the form of the buildings or bridges. They have even wrapped natural features such as cliffs.

The Gates was a project for a series of thresholds or portals that marched through Central Park in New York. The project was first envisioned in 1979 and it took over 25 years for the project to come to fruition. The rectangular structure of the individual units intentionally reflected the orthogonal and geometric grid pattern of the surrounding city blocks. However, the organic and flowing arrangement of the gates was conceived as a reaction to this order. The saffron-coloured poles and free-flowing nylon panels were reminiscent of trees blowing in the wind. There were an amazing 7,503 gates installed, which were spaced at 3.65-metre intervals. They were all 4.87 metres tall, but ranged in width from 1.68–5.48 metres.

The installation lasted for just 16 spectacular days; then the work of art was removed and recycled.

Top:
Central Park
The gates are a colourful contrast to the icy winter grey of the parkland.

Above:
Organisation
The installation took over 25 years to organise and was in place for just 16 days.

Facing page:
Detail
The intrinsic order of the gates is broken by the free-flowing fabric.

Autonomous objects: stand alone

Objects and elements can be conceived and constructed in one of two ways. The object can be designed from scratch, in that all the individual parts of the element are carefully collected together, then fashioned and constructed. The dimensions and style may or may not be specific to the particular location. This process is described as bespoke. The second approach is off the peg, objects that are constructed from an assembly of found or readily available elements. This may still create a new complete installation that is responsive to its particular position. It is the method of construction that differentiates the two approaches.

Name:
Turning the Place Over
(see pp 154+155)

Location:
Liverpool, England

Date:
2008 (temporary work)

Designer:
Richard Wilson

Bespoke

Objects that are created from specifically fashioned parts can be described as bespoke. The individual components are specially manufactured for the specific object. The designer will conceive of every constituent and feature of the complete object and pass the construction drawings to the manufacturer, who will then make the object. The designer has exact control over the finished object. Examples of this type of element include seats, exhibition and display stands and fitted furniture.

Off the peg

Elements that are made from readily available parts can be described as off the peg. The designer will create an object with the full knowledge of what is readily obtainable. They will be aware of the dimensions and types of materials that can be easily used. Off-the-peg elements are often created from what could be described as a kit of parts from which the designer can choose. Examples of this type of process include fitted kitchens and bathrooms, office furniture and soft furnishings.

Facing page:
Crate House, Massachusetts, USA (see pp162+163).

Elements that are designed to occupy a specific position within a given location can reflect the overall design concept of the complete interior. A small element within a large space can reveal and display the ideas that are guiding complete design. The details can be a small part of the overall strategy, but the consideration that is given to their design is as important as that given to the planning and organisation of the space.

Facing page:
Shop window
The cantilevered exhibition stand (once used to display typewriters) appears to hover behind the glass façade.

Below:
Shelf detail
The elegant stand springs from the window frame – note the vertical aluminium support to the rear of the display stand.

Olivetti showroom

Name:
Olivetti showroom

Location:
Venice, Italy

Date:
1958

Designer:
Carlo Scarpa

Carlo Scarpa is regarded by many as the designer who changed the overriding attitude towards the design of interiors. He emerged from the era of modernism and the approach that buildings should be replaced and rebuilt rather than remodelled. He placed great importance upon tradition, context and the enhancement of what was already there.

The renovation of a showroom on St Mark's Square in Venice, for typewriter manufacturers, Olivetti, was a relatively early project for Carlo Scarpa. His approach was to both accentuate the length of the shop and emphasise the light in the barely double-height space. He placed a U-shaped wooden balcony within the single room of the shop. This was accessed by an elongated marble staircase, which seems to flow into the body of the room. As always, through the use of upstands and gullies, Scarpa created a connection with the ever-present threat of water in Venice.

The typewriters were displayed in the windows on specially designed exhibition stands. Now used to display works of art, these appear to spring directly from the window itself. The seemingly cantilevered object is supported first upon turned stainless steel rods, which are attached to a bent angular bronze frame. This in turn supports fixings that allow the horizontal wooden exhibition surface to have the appearance of hovering above the frame. Further support is taken from the vertical steel rods that hang from the ceiling.

Scarpa has designed an intricate object that not only reflects the qualities of its context (Venice, the showroom), but also the complex nature of the typewriters that were once exhibited in the space.

Kolumba Museum

Name:
Kolumba Museum

Location:
Cologne, Germany

Date:
2008

Designer:
Peter Zumthor

Peter Zumthor is a highly influential and well-regarded architect. He creates buildings that connect with their situation, that seem appropriate to their surroundings; they have the quality of appearing to be newly constructed while also giving the impression of always having been there. This was his approach to the Kolumba Museum for Religious Art in Cologne, which meshed old and new, ancient and modern to create a timeless and evocative building.

The new building is placed directly upon the ruinous walls of an old church. The junction between old and new is not celebrated, it is simply there; the two butt up against each other. The single material of the wall, a light grey brick, rises in line with the existing building. It is delicately textured, the mortar is unusually thick and, in places, bricks are missing to allow light to filter in and out of the building. The bricks are narrow, just 36mm high, and of varying length up to 520mm long. These were specially developed for the project by Peterson, a Danish company. These custom-made elements reinforce the connection that the building has with the site and with earth.

The Kolumba Museum is both heavy and light; it appears to float above the ruins but also be strongly rooted to the ground. The remodelling and adaptation of the original church building creates a new museum that is a statement about context, permanence, tradition and ritual. It is a building that is evocative and emotional, established and contemporary, while also being entirely appropriate.

Left:
Courtyard
Elements of the old building are exposed and presented as exhibits.

Constructing objects

Above:
The archaeological site
The new circulation hovers above
the ruins in this cavernous interior.

Right:
Exterior
The new walls absorb the ruins
of the previous building.

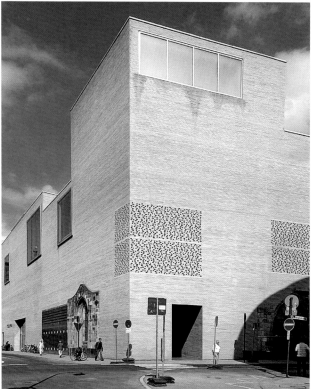

Above:
View through interior
Translucent glass is used to diffuse light and generate atmosphere in the restaurant.

Facing page:
The bar
The bespoke stools reinforce the linear quality of the long, elegant counter.

David Archer Architects have an obsession with detail. They control the design of an object from the conception to installation. When creating a specific element, the architects will update and correct the manufacturer's drawings and maquettes until they are certain that the design is perfect. This is a lengthy process involving many different sets of drawings and hours of effort and discussion.

Aaya restaurant

Name:
Aaya restaurant

Location:
London, England

Date:
2008

Designer:
David Archer Architects

Aaya is a Japanese restaurant in the heart of Soho, London. The space is organised in an orthogonal manner, which reflects the rigid order of the enclosing space. The restaurant is arranged over two floors, which don't quite overlap. The ground floor is almost square, while the basement is much bigger; it is long and thin and also contains the kitchens. Japanese-inspired screens further divide the space, thus creating a restaurant that has many different qualities of intimacy and atmosphere.

The majority of the elements that inhabit the restaurant are modest, unpretentious and low. However, the bar, which is situated on the ground floor at the opposite side of the room to the entrance, is one enormous element that sweeps all the way across the restaurant. It dramatically dives through the space linking the window with the back wall. The strength of this element is reinforced by the carefully designed bar stools that line up next to it and the oversized lamps that illuminate it from above. The long bar is slightly higher than the rest of the furniture in the room, and that small amount of extra height allows it to control, overlook and bring together the complete interior.

Constructing objects

Above:
The moving storyboard wall
The screen can swing into the centre of the room to create an intimate space behind it.

Left:
Main space
The warm, top-lit room is lined with Douglas fir. Note the intimate booth set into the wall.

Facing page:
Detail
A tableau representing scenes from Scottish history.

'The oral tradition is strong in northern European cultures in general and Scotland in particular, through the great Gaelic traditions, Border Ballads, Travellers' Tales and elsewhere. It is an inclusive and integrative artform embracing literature and performance.'

Edinburgh Architecture

Scottish Storytelling Centre

Name:
Scottish Storytelling Centre

Location:
Edinburgh, Scotland

Date:
2006

Designer:
Malcolm Fraser Architects

Malcolm Fraser Architects are known for their contemporary, highly-crafted buildings. Their work respects tradition while seeking a simplicity that is based in modernism and is deeply rooted in the physical and cultural context.

The Storytelling Centre occupies an extraordinary site within the historic John Knox House. It is situated on the Royal Mile and is really the medieval gateway into Edinburgh. The building actually protrudes into the road, deliberately narrowing it and thus creating a degree of control over those entering and leaving the city.

The front of the building is tall and slightly imposing, it merges well with the cityscape of slightly foreboding and impenetrable structures. However, the journey through the interior is one of moving from the dark into the light. The building opens up, embracing the fall in the site and the courtyard beyond. This is reinforced by the illumination that is provided by the roof light and the full-height windows at the rear of the structure. The main gathering area at the back is a large, warm, double-height, timber-lined room.

The café occupies the lower area at the front, leaving the larger open space for performance and other activities. The walls are decorated with children's paintings, acts of installation art and an astonishing tableau of Scottish storytelling. This montage of small scenes is set into a moving wall; a room divider that is constructed from a grid of boxes, each with a different scene or story contained within it. It is formed from Douglas fir boards around a steel frame that cantilevers from a hinge at one end. This screen can swing into the space, thus creating a small, intimate area behind it. This secret and cosy little space is perfect for listening to the most horrible and scary of stories.

Right:
Section
This drawing shows how the main performance space is integrated into the existing building.

Below:
Stairs
Looking up through the stack of perforated, semi-transparent stairs.

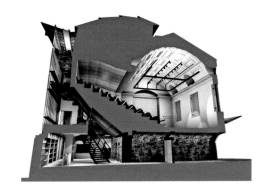

Stirling Tolbooth Arts Centre

Name:
Stirling Tolbooth Arts Centre

Location:
Stirling, Scotland

Date:
2001

Designer:
Richard Murphy Architects

A designer can add a single complex element to an existing building in order to activate the place. A unit can provide for all the functional activities necessary to facilitate the smooth running of the building without compromising the historical identity of the original structure.

The Stirling Tolbooth Arts Centre is a complex of buildings dating from the seventeenth century onwards. The old tolbooth had previously had many different functions, including the town hall, the courthouse and the jail. Richard Murphy Architects were commissioned to renovate the collection of structures as a music-focused arts venue, thus opening the building up to the local community and the wider public for performance and participation. The existing building, which occupies a prominent position within the city, was u-shaped; the courthouse occupied the central section with the vaults underneath. It was important not to interfere with the A-listed building as much as possible and so ensure that the elevations to the public streets and the fine interiors retained their character.

The approach that the designers took was to ensure that the distinctive interiors within the existing building were reserved for special uses, so that the old courtroom was reused as the performance space, the robing room as a grand bar and the old council chamber as a high-quality restaurant. The major intervention was reserved for the only empty space within the structure, the courtyard at the rear of the building. Into this tight, restricted space, the designers inserted what they describe as a 'backpack'. This contains an extension to the courtroom, which creates the auditorium and the air-handling plant. The extension also enclosed the courtyard from above, thus weatherproofing it. Into this space, the foyer and circulation systems were placed. As such, the designers have used a single, very complex element to activate the new use of the building.

Above:
The roof space
The new addition covers
a courtyard to create new
internal area.

Richard Murphy Architects

The practice established itself by designing small-
scale extensions to houses and mews conversions,
but have found its greatest success by creating
buildings for the arts. Richard Murphy Architects'
work is very influenced by Carlo Scarpa, in its
desire to create contemporary architecture but
with a sense of place and history.

Introduction > **Bespoke** > Off the peg

'To make a sculpture in the Turbine Hall at Tate Modern is an enormous challenge. The space is like no other – gargantuan and enveloping. I hope to challenge the space by developing a degree of intimacy, which somehow relates to all our lives.'

Rachel Whiteread

Embankment

Name:
Embankment

Location:
London, England

Date:
2005 (temporary work)

Designer:
Rachel Whiteread

Rachel Whiteread is one of the UK's leading contemporary sculptors. She has completed work all over the world, including the Holocaust Memorial in Vienna and Monument, which was displayed on Trafalgar Square's empty plinth. She was awarded the Turner Prize in 1993 for *House*.

Whiteread is known for the casts that she makes of the insides of familiar objects, these expose or seemingly make vulnerable and thus represent the objects in a different, unfamiliar manner. Rachel Whiteread's sculpture *Embankment* began with an old, worn cardboard box. Whiteread was going through her mother's belongings shortly after she died, when she came upon a box she remembered well. It had had many lives: it used to reside in her toy cupboard next to piles of board games and was filled with Christmas decorations at another point.

Over time, its sides started to collapse, the printed logo on the outside faded and the lid came to shine with the traces of all the Sellotape used to bind it up over the years. Although the inspiration for this project came from a particular box, Whiteread used many different shaped and sized containers to actually construct this piece. For the Turbine Hall, she created a gigantic labyrinth-like structure, made from 14,000 casts of the inside of different boxes, stacked to occupy this monumental space.

This installation discussed what may or may not have been in the sealed boxes; it talked of the futility of storing things, when they can't be seen and also examined the ideas of memory and association.

Facing page:
The Turbine Hall
The mountainous landscape of boxes.

Far left:
The stack
The crates were arranged in a formal manner reminiscent of a storage depot.

Left:
The mound
The casual arrangement of objects gave the installation an organic quality.

Constructing objects

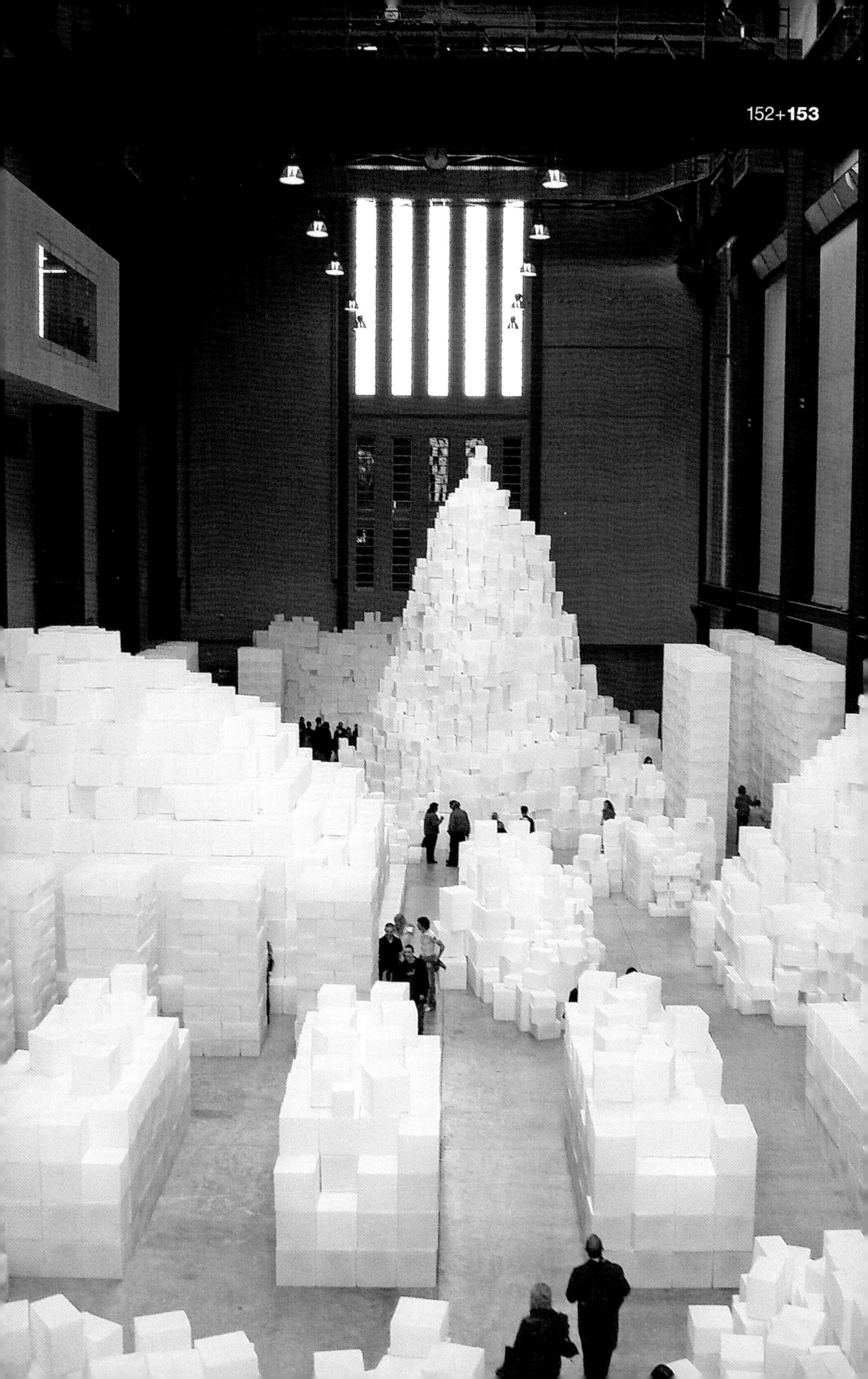

Turning the Place Over

Name:
Turning the Place Over

Location:
Liverpool, England

Date:
2008 (temporary work)

Designer:
Richard Wilson

Site-specific installation art is particularly relevant to the designers of interiors. The installation artist will often approach the project in a similar manner to that of the designer. They are both working with the existing, responding to what is already there. Sometimes, the only real difference is the designer will need to accommodate the functional requirements of the new users.

As part of the Year of Culture celebrations, Liverpool invited many artists, designers and architects to create site-specific installations around the city. Richard Wilson was asked to respond to the disused Yate's Wine Lodge, situated on the edge of the city centre. For *Turning the Place Over*, Wilson removed a huge, oval section of the façade of the building. This freed the disc from the structural and physical constraints of the wall. This section was then carefully supported so that it could rotate within its own cavity or cut out space.

This rotation was not quite true, so although the disc began in line with the façade, as it turned it appeared to float free from its constraints, becoming almost perilously horizontal at the peak of the rotation. The cut element was seven metres wide and weighed six-and-a-half tons. It was mounted on a rotating 11-metre-long spindle; this was attached back to a reinforced frame, which was in turn pinned to the structural frame of the building.

The installation discussed the impermanence and narrowness of the façade, the barriers that are created by walls and the links that can be established between inside and outside.

Above:
The moving façade element
The moving façade element rotates within its own cavity.

Richard Wilson

Richard Wilson became known for the installation *20:50*, an artwork that filled one room of the Saatchi Gallery in London with dark, shiny, incredibly pungent sump oil. The visitor was able to stand in the centre of the piece, at the heart of the installation. They were encouraged to meditate upon the highly reflective surfaces of the oil, the quality of the space that they were inhabiting and the dangerous and dirty nature of the material.

The reuse of readily available elements can change the viewer's perception of an object. The act of removing something from its natural or obvious location and placing it in an incongruous position could be regarded as radical and destructive. Conceptual artists have been appropriating objects for their own use for over a century and the designers of interiors are now using the same approach. Even now, at the beginning of the twenty-first century, it is still regarded as a pretty radical act.

Fountain

Name:
Fountain

Location:
N/A

Date:
1917

Designer:
Marcel Duchamp

Marcel Duchamp is credited with the first use of the 'readymade' object as a work of art. He created artworks by appropriating a mundane utilitarian object such as a bottle rack or a urinal and placing it in an art gallery. This very act of placement, of removing the object from its normal situation and introducing it into the rarefied atmosphere of the gallery, changed the viewer's perception of the object. It had become a work of art, because the artist, Duchamp, had declared it to be a work of art.

These readymades deliberately provoked the art world in a number of ways, not least by removing the human hand, or the craft, from the creative or production process. The exhibit that really shocked the most was *Fountain*, which Duchamp showed at the Society of Independent Artists Annual Exhibition in 1917. He submitted the mass-produced ceramic urinal, which was placed on its side, under the name 'R Mutt' (this was hastily painted on the piece just before it was shown). Apparently *Fountain* was covered up during the show and allegedly thrown out with the rubbish after the exhibition.

Ironically, after this most ignoble beginning, *Fountain* was reproduced by Duchamp in the 1960s as a series of authorised 'Multiples'. These can now be seen in galleries across the world.

Facing page:
The 'readymade'
Still a shocking conceptual statement, almost a century after it was first exhibited.

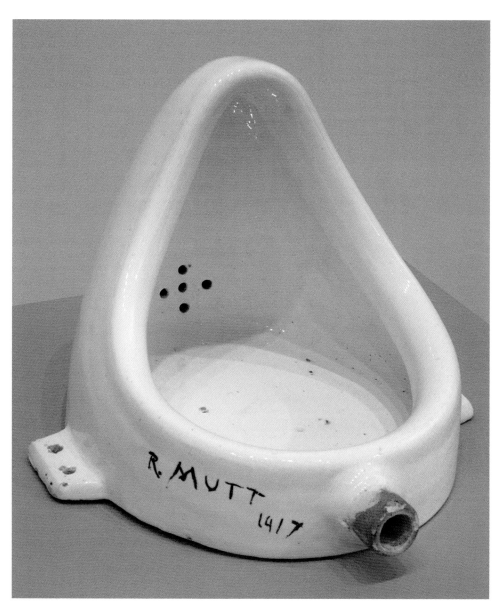

Duchamp's influence
In a poll of 500 renowned artists and historians, conducted by the BBC in 2004, Marcel Duchamp's *Fountain* was declared to be the most influential artwork of the twentieth century.

'The restitution of the fragments to a certain degree of wholeness within the larger program calls attention to another occurring, and consummately Venetian, concern: to create a density of time within their major monuments through the employment of rediscovered relics.'

Patricia Fortini Brown

Above:
Detail of steps
The reclaimed elements are quite crudely used.

Facing page:
The pulpit
The structure of the church frames the free-standing object.

Santa Maria Assunta Cathedral

Name:
Santa Maria Assunta Cathedral

Location:
Venice, Italy

Date:
Ninth–twelfth century

Designer:
Unknown

'Spolia' is an archaic term used to describe the recycling of existing architectural elements by incorporating them into new buildings. It is derived from the Latin word 'spoils', a phrase used to describe the act of taking trophies, usually armour and weaponry, from the enemy after a battle. Spolia is also a contemporary tactic and an integral element of the process of creating interior design; it is a method that is used by many contemporary interior architects and designers. The appropriation of elements from different sources, the reuse of details or fragments from other contexts, sampling, specifying and selecting key elements to be incorporated into a new design, are all fundamental skills in the armoury of an interior designer. The act of creating interior compositions composed of a selection of elements is an elemental skill.

On the small Venetian island of Torcello is the Santa Maria Assunta Cathedral. The island was the first to be populated and, for a while, was the most important. The cathedral was reconstructed in the ninth century, but was really abandoned in the thirteenth century as the growth of Venice, the silting up of its canals and the onset of malaria all helped to decimate its population. The cathedral pulpit is fabricated from *spolia*. Its steps are made from a series of reliefs that have been sawn and cut to provide an edge and balustrade to the stair. The carvings are datable to the eleventh and twelfth centuries and subsequent research uncovered the fact that they were dedicated to Kairos. In Torcello, the carvings were brutally treated. They were just cut to fit the steps and then edged with a reclaimed frieze detail, yet they were retained for their residual meaning; their connection to time. The pulpit was constructed from fragments, chunks or sections of old buildings. These readily available sections were reused in an economical yet sympathetic manner and their reuse creates a sense of continuity with the past.

Top:
Detail
A landscape of
architectural models.

Above:
Lighting
The exhibition is constructed from
crude and raw elements; naked
light bulbs and unfinished timber.

Facing page:
I Was There
The display stands dance
precariously through the space.

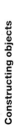

Constructing objects

I Was There

Name:
I Was There
(Chilean Pavilion at the
11th Venice Biennale)

Location:
Venice, Italy

Date:
2008 (temporary work)

Designer:
Alejandro Aravena, Eduardo
Castillo, José Cruz, German
del Sol, FAR Frohn & Rojas,
Sebastian Irarrazaval, Mathias
Klotz, Alberto Mozo, Cecilia Puga,
Smiljan Radic

The 11th Architecture Biennale
in Venice was entitled 'Out There:
Architecture Beyond Building'.
Aaron Betsky, who intended
to challenge the participants to
represent, shape and perhaps
even offer critical alternatives
to the human-made environment,
directed the Biennale. The two
main exhibition spaces were the
Biennale gardens, on the southern
tip of the island, and the Cordiere,
the vast rope-making sheds
of the Venice Arsenale. Within
the depths of the Cordiere was
the installation *I Was There*, the
Chilean pavilion.

The designers' response to
the theme of the exhibition
took the form of a huge number
of freestanding, roughly crafted
plinths, all raised to the same
eye level on slender timber legs.
These delicate and vulnerable
objects were closely placed
together within the cavernous
hall. A small ceramic model
of Chile's diverse and colourful
architecture was placed on top
of each plinth. These included
representations of old churches
and small thatched houses right
through to Brutalist office blocks
and contemporary cultural
buildings. Each naive model
and crate was illuminated by
a bare bulb, which was hung on
a long wire from the tall ceiling.
The viewer was invited to look
across the landscape of different
models as though they were
viewing a cityscape of miniature
buildings. The collection of
charming models of traditional
and contemporary architecture
encouraged the viewer to
reflect upon the enticing range
of experiences that this small
country has to offer.

Above:
The house
The crates plug into and slide out of the central element as and when requested.

Right:
Living room
Each crate is meticulously packed with technological equipment.

Facing page:
Bedroom
The bed is adaptable. It can be used as a settee or to sleep on.

> 'A room can act as a projection of personality and/or lifestyle, and can even represent aspects of character: a room is always greater than the sum of its material parts.'
>
> **Louise Ward**

Crate House

Name:
Crate House

Location:
Massachusetts, USA

Date:
1991 (temporary work)

Designer:
Allan Wexler

A single, well thought-out object can provide for all the living needs of a human being. These can be distilled into a few fundamental requirements, which can be collected together in a compact and concise manner.

In the White Cube Gallery on the campus of the University of Massachusetts, the architect and artist Allan Wexler was invited to participate in the creation of an installation intended to propose a living space that captured the essence of the 1990s. The structure was a stripped-down movable crate, with the essential functions of a dwelling pared back to their basic requirements. Bedroom, bathroom, kitchen and living room were treated as huge drawers on wheels that slid in and out of a central room as and when required.

Like a huge puzzle, each compartment within the crate was a compacted, essential version of a room, to be slid out of the crate and into the surrounding space. It was equipped with everything its occupant needed, although ironically, when everything was required and pulled into the central space, the space was no longer usable and the occupant was locked out. Allan Wexler on his website described his approach: 'Architecture insulates us from the cold, air conditions the heat, provides lots of ceiling height, even offers automatic coffee makers programmed to prepare coffee when we awake. I am more interested in discomfort.'

Crate House is a piece of installation art, but it also proposes a viable approach to the twenty-first century problems of overcrowding and city sprawl.

Right:
The office
View through the reception area. The meeting room on the right is a striking element within the space.

Below:
The container
The crate began its life in a goods yard before it was shipped to the fabricators to be transformed.

Reactor Film Studio

Name:
Reactor Film Studio

Location:
Los Angeles, USA

Date:
1996

Designer:
Pugh and Scarpa

The reuse of an off-the-peg element can greatly enhance the atmosphere and quality of a space. It can add a sense of nostalgia and remembrance to what would otherwise be a fairly anodyne place, or it can add contrast to an eclectic collection of elements and spaces. An off-the-peg element may be totally suitable for the interior, but from a different era or culture; it would then become subtly prominent. It could also be totally alien to the space and utilised as a dramatic statement or critique of the space.

The 1930s art deco garage has been transformed to house the new offices for Reactor Films, a media production company. Pugh and Scarpa installed a steel shipping container, in the front window of the building, to create a dramatic and dynamic meeting room. It was carefully positioned to engage with the street – the shipping container-turned-conference room obviously elicits curiosity from passers by. The treatment of the surrounding interior of the office space provides a discrete but complementary backdrop. The crate was opened up and altered so that it can accommodate its new function of meeting and conference room. Steps up to the raised floor were installed, openings cut into the walls and the box was lined for acoustic comfort.

The reuse and presentation of a found object and the placement of it in an unfamiliar position is an act that Marcel Duchamp championed at the beginning of the twentieth century. It is a process that produces productive results for the designers of interiors.

'A familiar thing seen in an unfamiliar context can become perceptually new as well as old.'

Robert Venturi

Below:
View of the meeting room
The simple, crude element has been enlarged and adapted to create a useful form.

'Their work is extraordinary and important – it questions architecture but also celebrates the potential of architecture.'

Paul Goldberger

'Tourisms: Suitcase Studies' exhibition

Name:
'Tourisms: Suitcase Studies' exhibition

Location:
Minneapolis, USA

Date:
1991 (temporary work)

Designer:
Diller Scofidio + Renfro

The repeated use of a single element can create a sense of uniformity and regulation. Once this has been established then it is fairly easy to introduce diversity; the standardisation will accentuate the miscellany or mixture, while the unusual will emphasise the ordinary.

This travelling exhibition was originally commissioned for the Walker Art Gallery in Minneapolis, Minnesota. 'Tourisms: Suitcase Studies' consisted of 50 charcoal grey Samsonite suitcases; each one represented a particular state of the USA. Every case contained a description and a commentary on a famous landmark within that state, it offered both official and unofficial observations, which took the form of postcards, texts and snapshots. Strangely, each 'Case Study' only examined two types of landmarks: famous battlefields and famous beds. These, the designers argued, are the two areas which are central to the development of 'aura', the key component and driving force upon which tourism is based. The cases were illuminated from within and hung from ceiling-mounted rods. The designers insisted that they were always installed in rows.

It was, of course, very easy for the curators, at the end of the scheduled exhibition, to pack it away and send it to its next destination.

Top:
Security x-ray photograph
Each exhibit is completely self-contained.

Above:
Suitcases
The identical elements are ready to be transported to the site of the next exhibition.

Constructing objects

Above:
View into the space
The exhibits are suspended from
the ceiling.

Right:
Detail of exhibit
Each case documents either
hotels or battlegrounds;
apparently the most popular
tourist destinations.

Bespoke > **Off the peg**

Facing page:
View through the cathedral
The red fabric is hanging from
the scaffolding, which is being
used to repair the building.

Installation at Our Lady's Cathedral, Tournai

Name:
Installation at Our Lady's
Cathedral, Tournai

Location:
Tournai, France

Date:
2008 (temporary work)

Designer:
Unknown

A single, everyday element that is
placed within an unusual context
can generate a dramatic and
emotional interior space. If vast
amounts of material or fabric are
used, the sheer quantity in itself
creates a theatrical display.

Tournai Cathedral is one
of the most beautiful religious
monuments in the Western
world. Due to the long time
that it took to build, it is actually
constructed in two different
styles, the Romanesque and
the Gothic. The majority of the
building, including the nave,
the transept and the five identical
bell towers, were built in the
twelfth century, while the ornate
choir was constructed in the
thirteenth century.

Every three years, Tournai
holds an international exhibition
dedicated to contemporary
textile creations. In 2008, the 6th
International Triennial of Textile
and Tapestry Arts celebrated the
links that the city has with Italy.
Installations were mounted in
all the major buildings, including
the Cathedral.

The building was undergoing
an extensive process of cleaning
and repair at the time of the
exhibition. The artist used this
as the basis of the approach
to the space. She draped
an enormous length of red fabric
through the nave of the church.
It was hung from the scaffolding
and stretched back and forth
through the cathedral between
the apse and the choir. This
streak of red sweeping through
the huge interior of the cathedral
represented the need for repair
and the damage that had been
inflicted on the building by a small
earthquake in the late 1990s;
a vivid and spectacular comment.

Top:
The nave
The red fabric sweeps through
the cathedral.

Above:
Hanging fabric
Light shines through the delicate
diaphorous material.

Bespoke > **Off the peg**

Many of the methods of organising and assembling interior space have been presented and a number of specialist terms introduced. These have been collected together in the following glossary to provide an easy reference section. While it is impossible to be exhaustive, a good number of the terms that are the common language and terminology of interior design and architecture today are shown.

Acoustics The scientific study of sound and sound waves. The particular acoustic properties of an interior can be manipulated through the use of sound-absorbent materials and fractured surfaces, both of which affect the reverberation time and reduce distortion and echo.

Adaptation The process of transforming an existing building to accommodate new uses. This is also referred to as remodelling, adaptive reuse and interior architecture.

Analysis The act of exploring and studying an existing building or context. There are a number of different methods that the designer can use to carry out this investigation. It is the understanding of the meaningful qualities of the building that can prompt or stimulate the process of transforming the space.

Art deco A style of design that proliferated throughout Europe and North America in the early 1900s. It was know for the use of dynamic diagonals and flamboyant colours. The name is derived from the Paris-based 1925 Exposition Internationale des Arts Décoratifs et Industriels Modernes.

Atrium Originally an atrium was an uncovered Roman courtyard, however the term is now commonly used to describe a covered interior space that usually has a glazed roof which allows sunlight and warmth to enter an interior.

Auditorium The area within a concert hall or theatre in which the audience sit.

Autonomous interior An interior space that is considered to be merely the container for the new use and which exerts little influence on the form and character of the new interior.

Axis An imaginary line that usually runs through the centre of a space or building, it is used as a planning device and is related to symmetry. Axial planning can be used to arrange an interior in balanced manner or in a way that prioritises certain qualities, such as a view through the space or a particular hierarchy.

Bespoke An object or interior that is constructed to occupy a particular position and is designed to satisfy the specific requirements of the user.

Canopy A covering erected to provide protection from the elements or to emphasise a particular activity. A canopy is often found at the entrance to a building, but it can also be a freestanding element within an open space.

Cantilever The process of extending a floor, balcony or other part of the building beyond the walls of the structure. The lack of any visible means of support gives this device a dramatic and slightly dangerous quality, however, structural support is provided by tying the cantilevered elements back to the bulk of the rest of the building.

Circulation The methods of movement within a building. Circulation is often arranged as a series of routes horizontally through a building via walkways, corridors and bridges, or vertically via stairs, ramps, lifts and escalators.

Classical Classical architecture derives its principles from Greek and Roman art and architecture. The main orders of classical architecture are Tuscan, Doric, Ionic, Corinthian and Composite. In its revived style, it is known as neo-classicalism.

Colonnade A devise for controlling movement and space, it consists of a series of regularly placed columns that support a roof.

Concept An abstract idea that can act as the generator for the design of an interior.

Conservation The act of preserving an existing structure. This encompasses the process of keeping it as it is, but preventing any further deterioration, or returning it to its original state, and also updating the building for contemporary use.

Contemporary The design philosophy that exists at the present time.

Context In interior architecture, the context consists of the conditions surrounding the building to be reused. These conditions may be in close proximity or far away and have a variety of impacts upon the new interior.

Courtyard An open space between, behind or within a building, it does not usually have a roof, that is, it is open to the elements but it is enclosed by walls.

Design process The design process is the method by which a new design is created and realised.

Detail The intimate examination of the particular joints and materials within an interior. This includes the application of materials and the manipulation of surfaces.

Element Within an interior, a specific object such as a piece of furniture or a room can be described as an 'element'.

Elevation An elevation is a drawing, usually of an outside wall or façade of a building. It is a two-dimensional representation of a wall showing the position of windows, doors and any other details of the building.

Ephemeral Generally refers to designs that are short lived or transitory. Interiors are often described as ephemeral because of their temporary quality.

Ergonomics The study of spatial relationships and proportions in relation to the human body. This is exemplified by the *New Metric Handbook*, a book that catalogues these relationships and sets out the 'standards' of ergonomic reasoning.

Façade Quite simply, the exterior front plane of a building.

Fitted furniture Elements within an interior that are designed and constructed to occupy a specific position. Within a domestic situation, the kitchen or bathroom could be described as fitted, but it is also a common tactic used in many different types of interior design.

Focal point A visual point within an interior that attention of activity is concentrated upon.

Form The shape or configuration of an element or space. Form is quite distinct and different to colour or texture.

Form follows form The notion that the design of an interior space is influenced by the qualities of the space in which it is being built.

Form follows function The modernist declaration that the design of new buildings and interior spaces is determined by the functions that happen within them.

Found object An object that has been removed from its natural situation and placed in an quite different context.

Found texture When working with existing buildings, found surfaces within the space can be retained and used to provide a meaningful connection to the history of the site.

Free plan A system of design that uses a framed structure, and thus removes the need for load-bearing walls. This creates a freedom and flexibility within the space.

Freestanding An element or object the is self-supporting, that is, something that takes no structural support from its immediate surroundings.

Function The actual use of a space, either new or old, will often be referred to as the function. It describes the activities that the end-users of the interior carry out within the space.

Furniture/furnishings The character of a particular room can be created by the furniture, which can either been custom made or selected by the designer. Soft furnishings describe the carpets, curtains, upholstery and other textile finishes.

Genius loci The particular and distinct 'spirit' of a place or building.

Geometry The field of studying the spatial relationships between things; closely related to mathematics. In architecture and design, it relates to the systematic organisation of building spaces and elements.

Hierarchy When organising and planning space, the phrase 'hierarchy' is sometimes used to distinguish primary and secondary elements within a design. It may also be used to classify major and minor functions within a space.

Holistic The consideration of every element in the design. Within the design of interiors, this may include other design disciplines such as graphics, textiles or product design.

Host building The original or existing building that is to be remodelled.

Interior architecture Interior architecture is the practice of remodelling existing buildings. As well as the robust reworking of a building, interior architecture often deals with complex structural, environmental and servicing problems. It is sometimes referred to as adaptation, adaptive reuse or remodelling.

Interior decoration Interior decoration is the art of decorating inside spaces and rooms to impart a particular character and atmosphere to the room. It is often concerned with such issues as surface pattern, ornament, furniture, soft furnishings and lighting.

Interior design Interior design is an interdisciplinary practice that is concerned with the creation of a range of interior environments that articulate identity and atmosphere, through the manipulation of spatial volume, the placement of specific objects and furniture, and the treatment of surfaces.

Intervention A procedure that activates the potential or repressed meaning of a specific place. It truly works when the architectural response of the designer is very sympathetic towards the existing building.

Insertion The placement of a complete object within the confines of an existing building. It is a practice that establishes an intense relationship between the original building and the inserted element and yet allows the character of each to exist in a strong and independent manner.

Installation The strategy of placing a series or group of related elements within the context of an existing building. This is a process that will heighten the awareness of an existing building without adversely affecting it.

Landmark A prominent object within a building or landscape.

Load bearing A term that refers to the structural system employed to construct the building. It refers to a structure that is usually masonry and built up, brick-by-brick, from the ground.

Louvre Thin horizontal planes that are usually fashioned from timber or steel and are placed on the outside of an opening to protect the interior from direct sunlight.

Materials The actual substances that are used to shape and order an interior. Commonly used materials are wood, glass, steel, plastic and stone, as well as textiles.

Modernism A movement in design, architecture and society that flourished between approximately 1900–1960, and which defined the modern world. Modernists developed what was to become known as the machine aesthetic, they argued that a sufficient level of perfection could be achieved in architecture, thus ensuring the ideal environment for human existence.

Narrative A story or a text. Within architecture and design, narrative can describe the concept or the sequence of events that the designer may wish to convey; the existing building, the exhibition design, the concept or the identity.

Object A purposefully placed object is loaded with meaning; whether it is a small piece of furniture, a large sculpture or a number of pieces clustered together, it establishes a physical and cultural relationship with its environment. Object and element are often interchangeable.

Occupation The manner in which a space is used; the function or inhabitation of an interior.

Off the peg An element, object or piece of furniture that is manufactured off-site. It is not designed to occupy a specific position, but is selected by the designer to be situated in a particular place.

Organisation The planning or arrangement of a space; that is placement of the objects, rooms and elements.

Orientation The direction in which a space is facing, used especially when a relationship is established between the interior and another object or feature.

Ornament A decorative detail than can be used to embellish parts of a building or an interior. It was often regarded as superfluous and it became a highly debated element of design in the twentieth century. However, within the early decades of the twenty-first century, it is becoming a much-used device.

Orthogonal The use of right angles within a design.

Pastiche An imitation of the style of an earlier period.

Patination Derived from the word 'patina', patination describes the change in the surface texture or pattern over time.

Plan libre See Free plan.

Plane The façade, wall, ceiling and floor are regarded as the essential 'planes' of the interior and a building.

Planning The organisation of an interior, that is the arrangement of the rooms, spaces and structure.

Playstation organisation An organisational technique where a collection of events or objects are arranged in series, each is a complete entity and has to be fully appreciated before it the viewer or competitor can move on, similar to the organisational technique used in PlayStation or other computer games.

Postmodernism A process of making reference to old forms and precepts, and mimicking building styles and techniques. Twenty-first century postmodern theory connects many areas associated with contemporary consumer culture, hyper-reality and anaesthetic architecture, and this results in an inevitable incoherence.

Programmatic requirements An understanding of the complex needs of the end-users of the building.

Promenade One of Le Corbusier's five-points of architecture, it is the modernist concept of continual movement through a building. This journey is also referred to as architectural promenade.

Raumplan (space plan) The Viennese architect Adolf Loos devised the Raumplan (space plan). It is best exemplified in the designs for the Müller and Moller houses in Prague and Vienna: the houses consist of a series of compact, enclosed and intimately connected rooms and movement between them often organised in a circular manner.

Readymade The development of art from utilitarian everyday found objects not normally considered as art in their on right. The term 'readymade' was coined by the artist Marcel Duchamp, who created a series of objet d'art from such items as a bicycle wheel, a bottle rack and a urinal.

Remodelling The process of wholeheartedly altering a building. The function is the most obvious change, but other alterations may be made to the building such as its structure, circulation routes and its orientation. Additions may be constructed while other areas may be demolished.

Responsive interiors The reading of an original space can present certain clues or pointers to the nature and character of the redesign. These types of new interiors are very sympathetic to the qualities of the existing building.

Reuse The transformation of an existing building may also be described as 'reuse'; a term that suggests that the elements and parts of both new and old building are reworked in order to create a new space. See also adaptation, remodelling and interior architecture.

Sarcophagus A stone or marble coffin, usually ancient with reliefs and inscriptions.

Scale The size of an element or object in relation to other objects or elements is referred to as its scale. Scale can also refer to the ratio of the size of an object or space to a drawing of that object or space. So, for example, a floor plan drawn at 1:100 scale, is 100 times smaller than the actual space.

Section At any point on the plan of a building, the designer may describe a line through the drawing and visualise a vertical cut through the spaces. This is called a section, it will explain the volumes of the spaces and indicate the position of the walls, the floors, the roof and other structural elements.

Sequence A term used to describe the order of interior spaces that the designer intends the visitor to experience in their journey through the space.

Site-specific The site is the specific location or context of a building or space. Site-specific is a phrase used to describe the influences that are derived directly from the particular conditions found on site.

Spolia The act of reusing building elements and applying them to new or later monuments. It derives from the phrase 'the spoils of war' where the victors in battle would take trophies from their foes.

Strategy The overall plan or proposal for the design of an interior.

Threshold The point of transition between two spaces, whether this is inside and outside or two interior spaces.

Truss A number of beams and/or rafters tied together to form a bridging element.

Urbanism The study of cities, their evolution and development.

View Usually the image of a scene, typically a pleasant picture, through an opening or from the building.

Acknowledgements

Graeme Brooker would like to thank
Fredo, Sylvain, Ben and Jasper for their
melodiousness, Shelley and Howard for their
civility and Claire for her graciousness.

Sally Stone would like to thank the
Miller Stevensons for their comradeship,
Reuben, Ivan and Agnes for their
ebullience and Dominic for his equanimity.

Both Graeme and Sally would like to thank
all of the designers and photographers who
have lent their work for publication and AVA
Publishing, especially Rachel Netherwood
and Leafy Robinson, for their persistent
encouragement throughout the project.

Elements/Objects

Images

All photographs © Graeme Brooker and Sally Stone, except for:

Cover image: courtesy of Pugh + Scarpa Architects
002: Courtesy of Bouroullec Brothers
007: Photograph by Timothy Soar
010: Photography by Roos Aldershoff www.roosaldershoff.com
013: Courtesy of Greg Epps, Ravensbourne College
015: Photograph by Sue Barr
016+017: Photography by Roos Aldershoff www.roosaldershoff.com; drawings courtesy of Merkx + Girod
018: Courtesy of Terry Meade, Brighton University
019: Courtesy of Greg Epps, Ravensbourne College
020+021: © Siftung Preussischer Kulturbesitz/David Chipperfield Architects, photographer: Ute Zscharnt
024+025: Photographs by Christian Richters
026+027: Photographs by Andrea Martiradonna
028+029: Courtesy of Walter Van Beirendonck
030+031: Photographs by Matteo Piazza; diagram by Lazzarini Pickering
032+033: Photograph by Katsuhisa Kida, courtesy of Klein Dytham Architecture
034+035: Photographs by Keith Collie
036+037: Courtesy of Ben Kelly Design
038+039: Photograph by Iwan Baan
040+041: Courtesy of Panter Hudspith Architects

044+045: Courtesy of Dominic Roberts
046+047: Courtesy of Panter Hudspith Architects
048+049: Photograph © Dennis Gilbert, courtesy of View Pictures Ltd; diagrams by Jamie Fobert Architects
052+053: Photographs © Keith Hunter
056+057: Photograph by Iwan Baan, diagram by Petra Blaisse
060+061: Photographs by Keith Collie
062+063: All images courtesy of John L. Johnson
065: Photographs by Christian Richters / Joerg von Bruchhausen
066+067: Photograph by Steve Greaves
068+069: Photograph courtesy of Behnisch Architekten
070+071: Photographs by Margherita Spiluttini
074+075: Photographs courtesy of Casson Mann
076+077: Photographs and drawings courtesy of Behnisch Architekten
078+079: Photographs by Marvin Rand; drawing courtesy of Pugh + Scarpa Architects
080+081: Photograph by Timothy Soar, courtesy of Arca
082+083: Photographs by Richard Bryant/arcaid.co.uk; drawing by Sarah Wigglesworth Architects
084+085: Photographs by Steve Greaves
086+087: Photographs courtesy of Francis Roberts Architects
088+089: Photographs and drawing courtesy of Paul Keogh Architects
090+091: Photographs and drawings courtesy of Malcolm Fraser Architects
094+095: Photograph courtesy of Johann Peter Luth
096+097: Photograph © Fotoworks / Benny Chan, courtesy of NMDA

098+099: Photographs courtesy of Casson Mann
102+103: Photographs courtesy of Diller Scofidio + Renfro
104+105: Photographs courtesy of Block Architecture
106+107: Photograph © Gerald Zugmann / www.zugmann.com; drawing courtesy of Coop Himmelblau
108+109: Photographs © Fotoworks / Benny Chan, courtesy of NMDA
112+113: Photographs by Edward Woodman
114+115: Photographs courtesy of Johann Peter Luth
116+117: Image courtesy of Softroom
118+119: Photograph by David Grandorge, courtesy of 6a Architects
124+125: Photographs courtesy of Bouroullec Brothers
126+127: Images courtesy of Softroom
128+129: Photograph © Victor S. Brigola / Artur, courtesy of View Pictures Ltd
130+131: Courtesy of Greg Epps, Ravensbourne College
132+133: Photograph (132) by Stephanie Macdonald; photograph (133) by David Grandorge, drawing by 6a Architects
140+141: Photograph courtesy of Allan Wexler
146+147: Photographs by Keith Collie
150+151: Photographs and drawing courtesy of Richard Murphy Architects
162+163: Photographs courtesy of Allan Wexler
164+165: Photographs courtesy of Pugh + Scarpa Architects
166+167: Photographs courtesy of Diller Scofidio + Renfro

Acknowledgements

Pull quotes

016: *Merkx + Girod website.* 2009. [online]. [Accessed 1st July 2009]. Available from World Wide Web: www.merkx-girod.nl
022: Betsky, A. *In: La Biennale di Venezia website.* 2009. [online]. [Accessed 1st July 2009]. Available from World Wide Web: www.labiennale.org/en/news/ architecture/en/80212.html
031: Scott, F. 2008. *On Altering Architecture.* London: Routledge
045: Aben, R. and de Wit, S. 1999. *The Enclosed Garden.* Rotterdam: 010 Publishers
047: Kent C., Bloomer, C., Moore, W. and Yudell, R.J. 1977. *Body, Memory and Architecture.* New Haven, CT: Yale University Press
051: Scarpa, C. In: Dal Co, F. and Mazzariol, G. 1984. Carlo Scarpa. Opera Completa. Florence: Electa
052: Cullen, G. 1971. *The Concise Townscape.* Oxford: Architectural Press
056: Milgrom, M. 2001. *OMA Earth Mother* [online]. [Accessed 1st July 2009]. Available from World Wide Web: www.metropolismag.com/html/ content_0401/milgrom/
059: Balmond, C. [source unavailable]
063: Kutich, J. and Eakin, G. 1993. *Interior Architecture.* Hoboken, NJ: Wiley

065: *World Architecture News website.* 2006. [online]. [Accessed 1st July 2009]. Available from World Wide Web: www.worldarchitecturenews.com /index.php?fuseaction= wanappln.projectview&upload_ id=652
073: Olsberg, N. 1999. Carlo *Scarpa Architect: Intervening with History.* New York, NY: Monacelli Press
074: Mann, R. 2001. In: *Casson Mann website.* [online]. [Accessed 1st July 2009]. Available from World Wide Web: www.cassonmann.co.uk/ exhibitions/great-expectations- press-release
091: *Malcolm Fraser Architects website.* 2009. [online]. [Accessed 1st July 2009]. Available from World Wide Web: www.malcolmfraser.co.uk/ projects/?contentid=257& parentid=248
092: Schittich, C. 2003. *Building in Existing Fabric.* München: Detail
101: Moore, M. 1992. *Blueprint Extra 04: Sackler Galleries.* Rowan Moore
109: Denari, M. 2008. *In: arcspace website.* [online]. [Accessed 1st July 2009]. Available from World Wide Web: www.arcspace.com/architects/ denari/hl23/hl23.html
113: Shone, R. 1995. *Rachel Whiteread House.* London: Phaidon
114: Ebert, Prof. Dr. W. 2008. *In: Weltkulturerbe Völklinger Hütte website.* [online]. [Accessed 1st July 2009]. Available from World Wide Web: www.voelklinger- huette.org/en/press-media/ news/202/

123: *Le Musée Jean Prouvé (1901–1984) website.* 2009. [online]. [Accessed 1st July 2009]. Available from World Wide Web: www.jeanprouve.com
124: Bouroullec, E. and Bouroullec, R. In: Zumstein, K. 2007. The Bouroullec Bond. *OnOffice.* March
133: [Author unknown]. 2006. *Financial Times.* 29th April
135: Walker, C. and Self, M. in conversation with the authors
136: *Christo and Jeanne-Claude website.* 2009. [online]. [Accessed 1st July 2009]. Available from World Wide Web: www.christojeanneclaude.net
149: Edinburgh Architecture website. 2009. [online]. [Accessed 1st July 2009]. Available from World Wide Web: www.edinburgharchitecture.co.uk /scottish_storytelling_centre.htm
152: Whiteread, R. [source unavailable]
159: Fortini Brown, P. 1996. *Venice and Antiquity.* New Haven, CT: Yale University Press
163: Ward, L. *In:* Sparke, P. and McKellar, S. (eds) 2004. *Interior Design and Identity.* Manchester: Manchester University Press
165: Venturi, R. 1977. *Complexity and Contradiction in Architecture.* New York, NY: Harry N. Abrams
166: Goldberger, P. *The New Yorker* [date unknown]

BASICS

INTERIOR ARCHITECTURE

Lynne Elvins
Naomi Goulder

Working with ethics

Publisher's note

The subject of ethics is not new, yet its consideration within the applied visual arts is perhaps not as prevalent as it might be. Our aim here is to help a new generation of students, educators and practitioners find a methodology for structuring their thoughts and reflections in this vital area.

AVA Publishing hopes that these **Working with ethics** pages provide a platform for consideration and a flexible method for incorporating ethical concerns in the work of educators, students and professionals. Our approach consists of four parts:

The **introduction** is intended to be an accessible snapshot of the ethical landscape, both in terms of historical development and current dominant themes.

The **framework** positions ethical consideration into four areas and poses questions about the practical implications that might occur. Marking your response to each of these questions on the scale shown will allow your reactions to be further explored by comparison.

The **case study** sets out a real project and then poses some ethical questions for further consideration. This is a focus point for a debate rather than a critical analysis, so there are no predetermined right or wrong answers.

A selection of **further reading** for you to consider areas of particular interest in more detail.

Introduction

Ethics is a complex subject that interlaces the idea of responsibilities to society with a wide range of considerations relevant to the character and happiness of the individual. It concerns virtues of compassion, loyalty and strength, but also of confidence, imagination, humour and optimism. As introduced in ancient Greek philosophy, the fundamental ethical question is *what should I do?* How we might pursue a 'good' life not only raises moral concerns about the effects of our actions on others, but also personal concerns about our own integrity.

In modern times the most important and controversial questions in ethics have been the moral ones. With growing populations and improvements in mobility and communications, it is not surprising that considerations about how to structure our lives together on the planet should come to the forefront. For visual artists and communicators, it should be no surprise that these considerations will enter into the creative process.

Some ethical considerations are already enshrined in government laws and regulations or in professional codes of conduct. For example, plagiarism and breaches of confidentiality can be punishable offences. Legislation in various nations makes it unlawful to exclude people with disabilities from accessing information or spaces. The trade of ivory as a material has been banned in many countries. In these cases, a clear line has been drawn under what is unacceptable.

But most ethical matters remain open to debate, among experts and lay-people alike, and in the end we have to make our own choices on the basis of our own guiding principles or values. Is it more ethical to work for a charity than for a commercial company? Is it unethical to create something that others find ugly or offensive?

Specific questions such as these may lead to other questions that are more abstract. For example, is it only effects on humans (and what they care about) that are important, or might effects on the natural world require attention too?

Is promoting ethical consequences justified even when it requires ethical sacrifices along the way? Must there be a single, unifying theory of ethics (such as the Utilitarian thesis that the right course of action is always the one that leads to the greatest happiness of the greatest number), or might there always be many different ethical values that pull a person in various directions?

As we enter into ethical debate and engage with these dilemmas on a personal and professional level, we may change our views or change our view of others. The real test though is whether, as we reflect on these matters, we change the way we act as well as the way we think. Socrates, the 'father' of philosophy, proposed that people will naturally do 'good' if they know what is right. But this point might only lead us to yet another question: *how do we know what is right?*

You
What are your ethical beliefs?

Central to everything you do will be your attitude to people and issues around you. For some people their ethics are an active part of the decisions they make everyday as a consumer, a voter or a working professional. Others may think about ethics very little and yet this does not automatically make them unethical. Personal beliefs, lifestyle, politics, nationality, religion, gender, class or education can all influence your ethical viewpoint.

Using the scale, where would you place yourself? What do you take into account to make your decision? Compare results with your friends or colleagues.

Your client
What are your terms?

Working relationships are central to whether ethics can be embedded into a project and your conduct on a day-to-day basis is a demonstration of your professional ethics. The decision with the biggest impact is whom you choose to work with in the first place. Cigarette companies or arms traders are often-cited examples when talking about where a line might be drawn, but rarely are real situations so extreme. At what point might you turn down a project on ethical grounds and how much does the reality of having to earn a living effect your ability to choose?

Using the scale, where would you place a project? How does this compare to your personal ethical level?

01 02 03 04 05 06 07 08 09 10

01 02 03 04 05 06 07 08 09 10

Your specifications
What are the impacts of your materials?

In relatively recent times we are learning that many natural materials are in short supply. At the same time we are increasingly aware that some man-made materials can have harmful, long-term effects on people or the planet. How much do you know about the materials that you use? Do you know where they come from, how far they travel and under what conditions they are obtained? When your creation is no longer needed, will it be easy and safe to recycle? Will it disappear without a trace? Are these considerations the responsibility of you or are they out of your hands?

Using the scale, mark how ethical your material choices are.

Your creation
What is the purpose of your work?

Between you, your colleagues and an agreed brief, what will your creation achieve? What purpose will it have in society and will it make a positive contribution? Should your work result in more than commercial success or industry awards? Might your creation help save lives, educate, protect or inspire? Form and function are two established aspects of judging a creation, but there is little consensus on the obligations of visual artists and communicators toward society, or the role they might have in solving social or environmental problems. If you want recognition for being the creator, how responsible are you for what you create and where might that responsibility end?

Using the scale, mark how ethical the purpose of your work is.

01 02 03 04 05 06 07 08 09 10

01 02 03 04 05 06 07 08 09 10

Working with ethics

One aspect of interior architecture that can raise an ethical dilemma is the issue of creating interior spaces that may directly affect peoples' emotions or behaviours. This might be done in positive or negative ways and often leads to a further question about who benefits from the emotions or behaviours that are created. For example, commercial retail interiors can be designed to slow people down and encourage them to follow certain paths in order to increase the chance of them making purchases; or a commercial office interior may be designed to improve productivity. At what point should (or do) projects such as these take into account the needs of the consumer or the worker? Is it a responsibility of the interior architect to factor-in the users of a space as well as the owners of a space, or are these considerations always in the hands of whoever funds the project?

Although London's Old Bailey has been rebuilt several times since 1674, the design of this courthouse remains largely the same. The accused stands in the dock directly facing the witness box and the judges are seated on the other side of the room. Jurors sit together so that they can consult with each other and arrive at their verdicts. Seated below the judges are clerks, lawyers and the writers who note the proceedings.

In 1673, the courtroom was opened up on one side. This was to increase the supply of fresh air to stop prisoners spreading typhus. Spectators crowded into the outside yard and their presence could influence or intimidate the jurors sitting inside. In 1737, the building was remodelled and enclosed – not only to keep out the weather, but also to limit the numbers of spectators.

In 1774, the court was rebuilt with luxurious facilities for court personnel and a separate room for witnesses was created so that they would not have to wait at a nearby public house. Such lavish provision for the judges and their servants contrasted dramatically with the prisoners' quarters in the basement.

Before the introduction of gas lighting in the early 19th century, a mirrored reflector was placed above the dock to reflect light on to the faces of the accused. This allowed the court to better examine facial expressions and assess their testimony.

A sounding board was also placed over their heads in order to amplify their voices. In some courtrooms (those in which prisoners were still branded), the interior included irons for holding convicts' hands while they were burnt.

A second courtroom was added in 1824. Reflecting the increasing role of lawyers, the new courtroom had seating for solicitors, counsel and law students. In 1841, both courtrooms were ventilated from chambers beneath the floors, filled with air drawn in from outside and propelled inside by a fan.

In 1877, it was decided to replace the courthouse with a larger building. It was adorned with symbolic reminders to the public of its virtuous purpose. Over the main entrance to the building was the carved inscription, 'defend the children of the poor and punish the wrongdoer'. Four oak-pannelled courtrooms contained space for all those who needed to attend modern trials. There were now separate rooms for male and female witnesses and another for witnesses of 'the better class'. Lawyers also had their own room, as did barristers' clerks.

The Old Bailey was heavily damaged by bombing in 1941 and then was subsequently rebuilt. A modern extension was added in 1972 but the current building, which is still England's most important crown court, remains essentially the same as the 1907 design.

Could the interior architecture of a courtroom affect the verdict?

Is it unethical to design an interior space to intimidate people?

Would you work on a courthouse project?

Rooms open into one another, everything communicates, and space is broken up into angles, diffuse areas and mobile sectors. Rooms, in short, have been liberalised.

Jean Baudrillard
The System of Objects

Working with ethics

Further reading

AIGA
Design business and ethics
2007, AIGA

Eaton, Marcia Muelder
Aesthetics and the good life
1989, Associated University Press

Ellison, David
Ethics and aesthetics in European modernist literature:
from the sublime to the uncanny
2001, Cambridge University Press

Fenner, David E W (Ed)
Ethics and the arts:
an anthology
1995, Garland Reference Library of Social Science

Gini, Al and Marcoux, Alexei M
Case studies in business ethics
2005, Prentice Hall

McDonough, William and Braungart, Michael
Cradle to cradle:
remaking the way we make things
2002, North Point Press

Papanek, Victor
Design for the real world:
making to measure
1972, Thames and Hudson

United Nations Global Compact
The ten principles
www.unglobalcompact.org/AboutTheGC/TheTenPrinciples/index.html